To my beloved parents, who have emba
journey beyond this world, yet whose spi
to guide and inspire me every d

For my father, who instilled in me the invaluable lesson that knowledge and wisdom are treasures so profound, that they remain forever untouchable by others' hands. Your wisdom lights my path, teaching me that the pursuit of understanding is the most noble journey one can undertake.

And for my mother, whose passion for the hues and luminance in Claude Monet's masterpieces opened my eyes to the endless beauty of the universe. You taught me to perceive the world in vibrant colours and soft lights, revealing the magic hidden in everyday moments.

This adventure through time and the essence of art is lovingly dedicated to both of you. Your lessons and love have shaped me into who I am, serving as my eternal inspiration and guiding light on my journey through life.

First Edition

ISBN: 978-1-0686042-0-1 (Paperback)
ISBN: 978-1-0686042-1-8 (ePub)

Cover design by Mario Gabbai

Acknowledgements

This book, a labour of love and creativity, has been brought to life with the support and encouragement of some incredibly special people. My deepest gratitude goes out to them for their invaluable contributions to this journey.

To my sister, Juliana Gabbai, whose sensibility and extensive experience with children's education have been instrumental in shaping this book. Juliana, your insights and passion for nurturing young minds have profoundly influenced the development of this story. Your guidance has helped me to create a narrative that is not only engaging but also educational and inspiring for children. Your belief in the importance of art in education has been a beacon of inspiration for me, and this book is a testament to the impact of your influence.

I also wish to extend my heartfelt thanks to Gemma Sharp for her invaluable input from a teacher's perspective. Gemma, your expertise and thoughtful feedback have enriched this book in countless ways. Your dedication to fostering a love for learning and creativity among children is truly admirable. Your suggestions and advice have been pivotal in ensuring that this book resonates with both children and educators alike.

To both Juliana and Gemma, your contributions have been a gift, and I am forever grateful for your support and wisdom. Thank you for being a part of this journey and for helping me bring this story to life. This book is a reflection of your passion and commitment to making a difference in the lives of children through education and art.

With warmest regards and endless gratitude,

Mario Gabbai

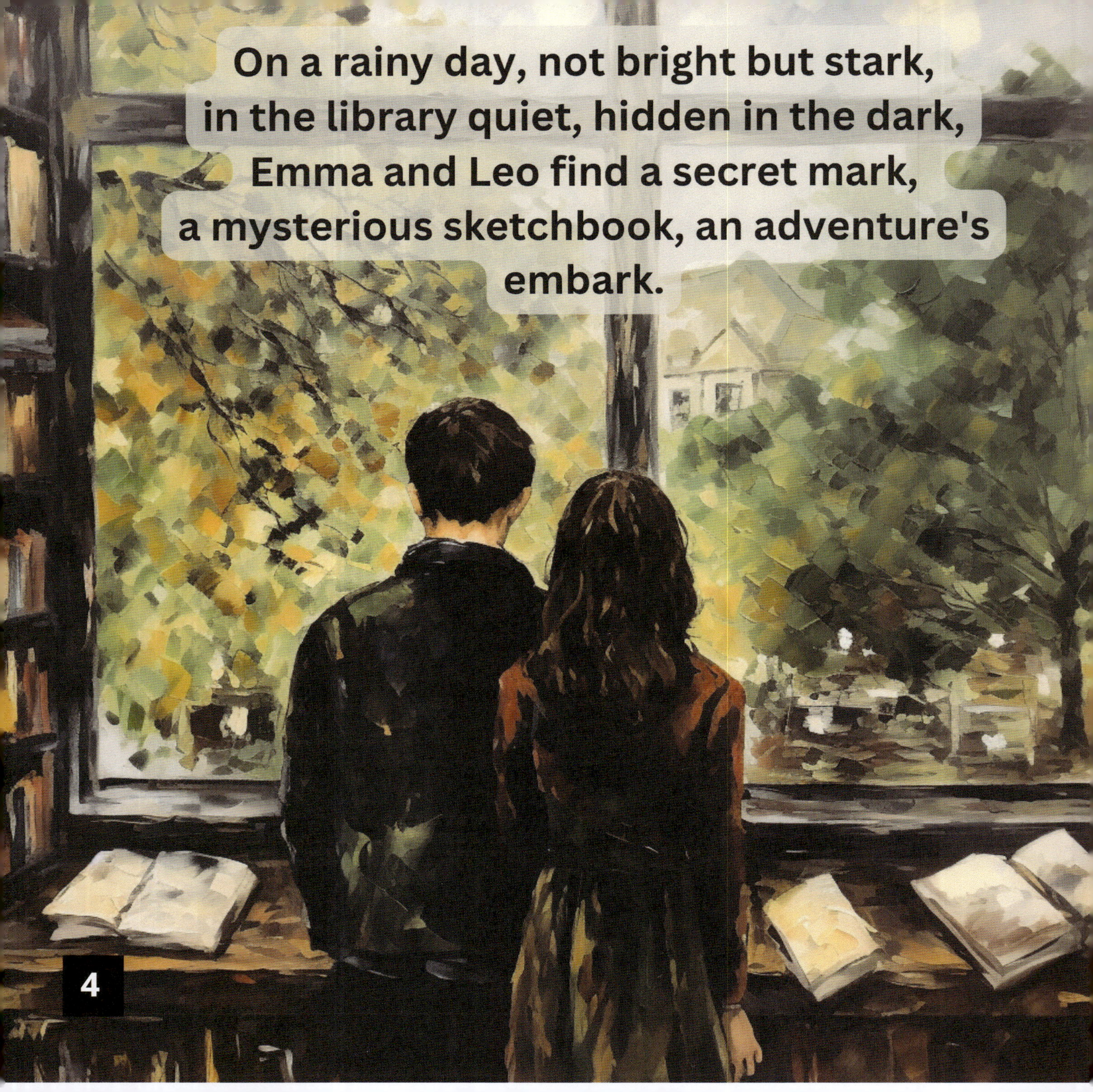

On a rainy day, not bright but stark,
in the library quiet, hidden in the dark,
Emma and Leo find a secret mark,
a mysterious sketchbook, an adventure's embark.

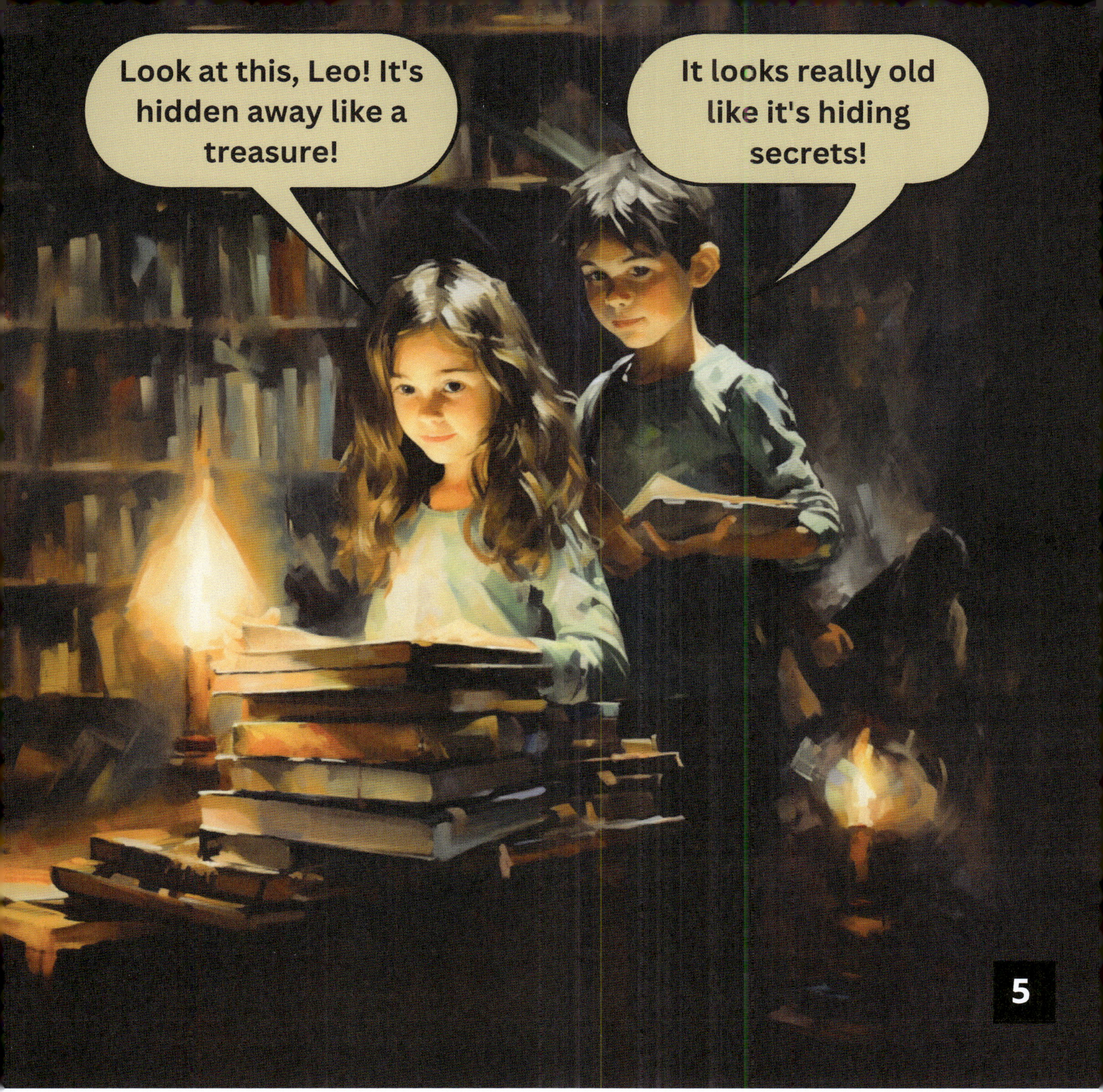
Look at this, Leo! It's hidden away like a treasure!
It looks really old like it's hiding secrets!

With gentle hands, Emma opens the find,
revealing pages of a mysterious kind,
a sketchbook of art, with tales entwined,
waiting for young minds to unwind.

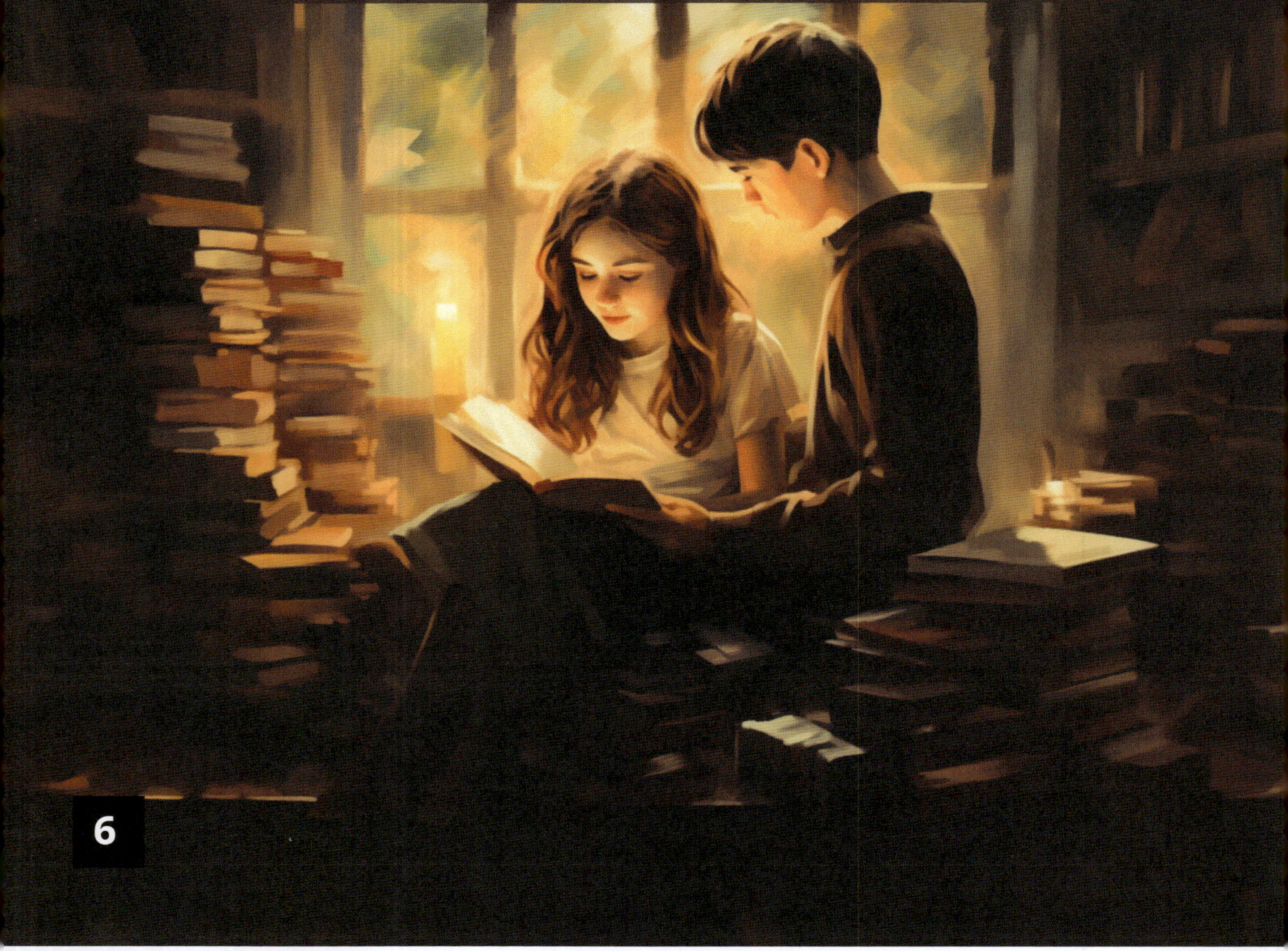

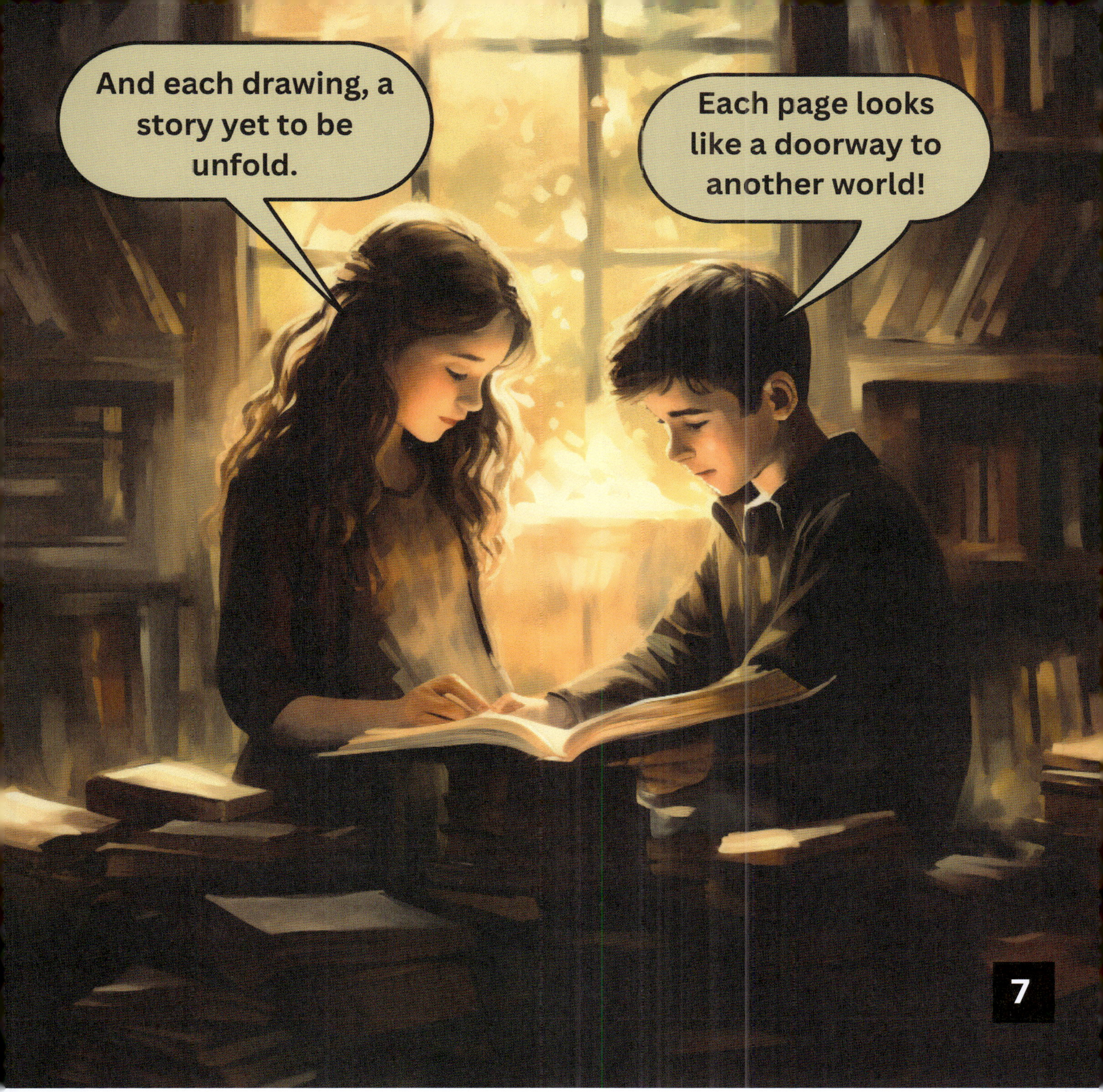
And each drawing, a story yet to be unfold.
Each page looks like a doorway to another world!

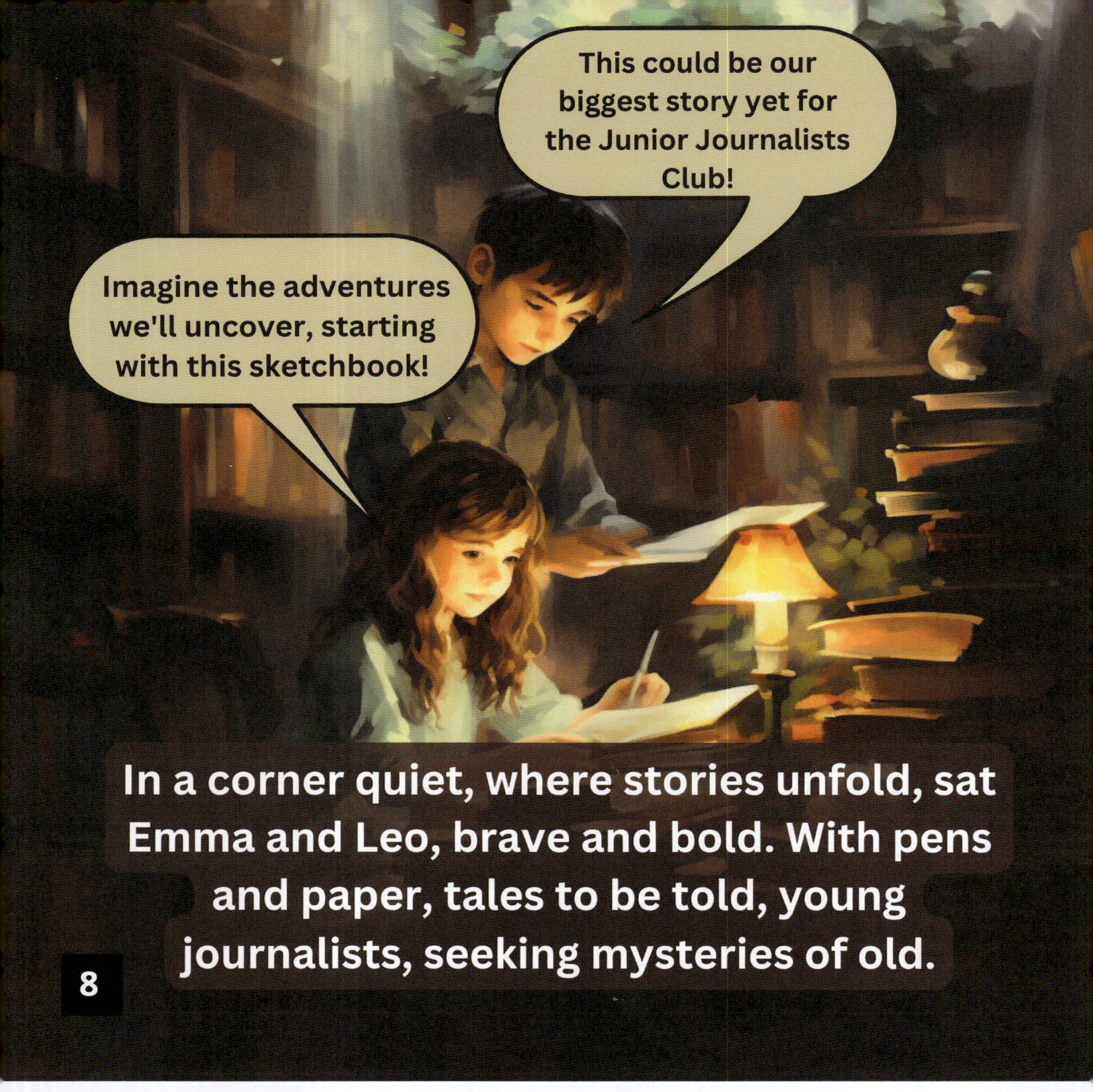

In a corner quiet, where stories unfold, sat Emma and Leo, brave and bold. With pens and paper, tales to be told, young journalists, seeking mysteries of old.

In this book of wonder, secrets tightly curled, now it's your turn, let your imagination unfold. Draw what you think the next page might hold, a story of magic, art, or adventures bold.

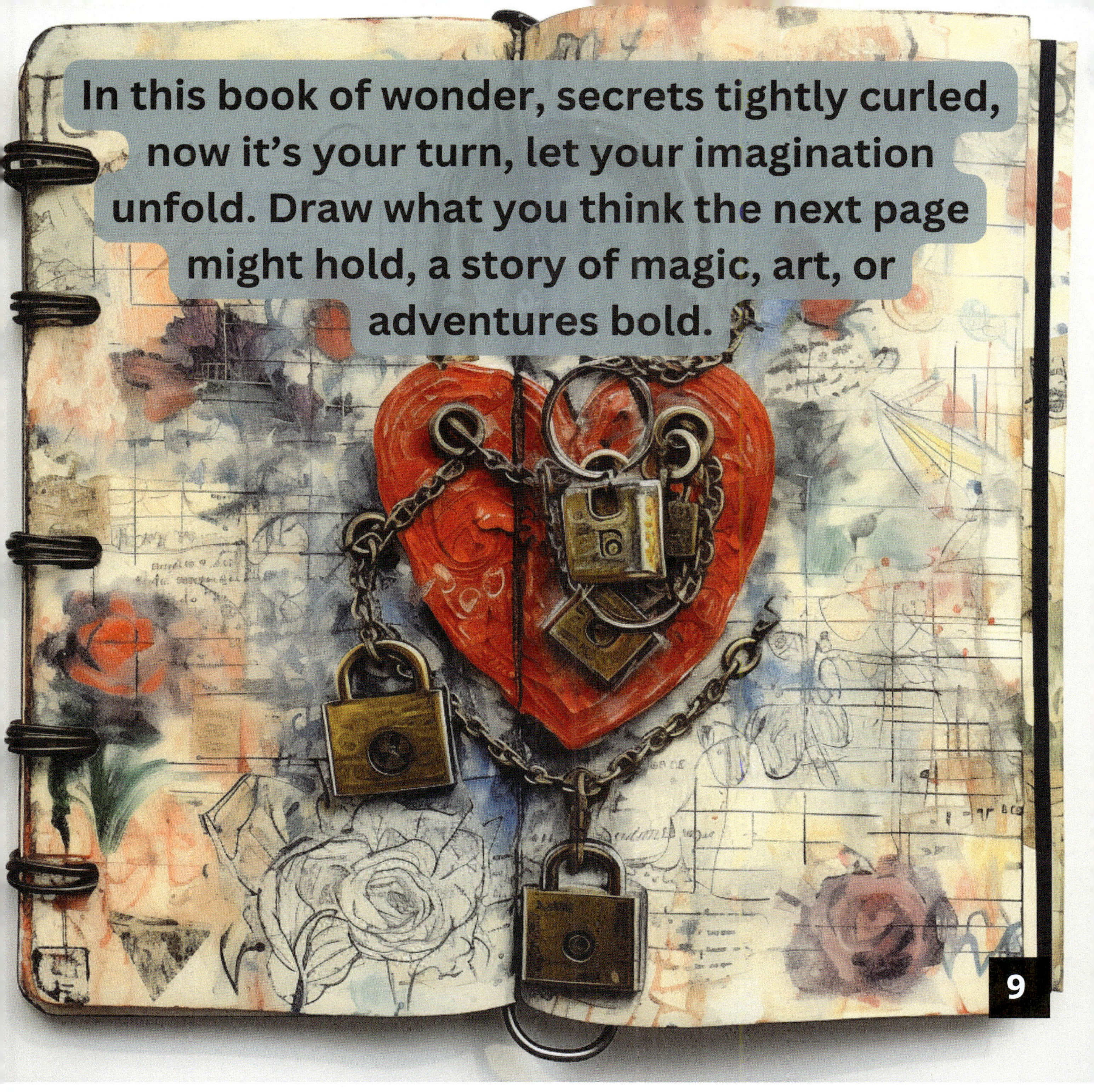

Draw here your interpretation of the next page of the sketchbook.

Turn the page, what do they see?
A garden of wonder, vibrant as can be,
with Lilies, ponds, and greenery free,
a magical place, they both agree.

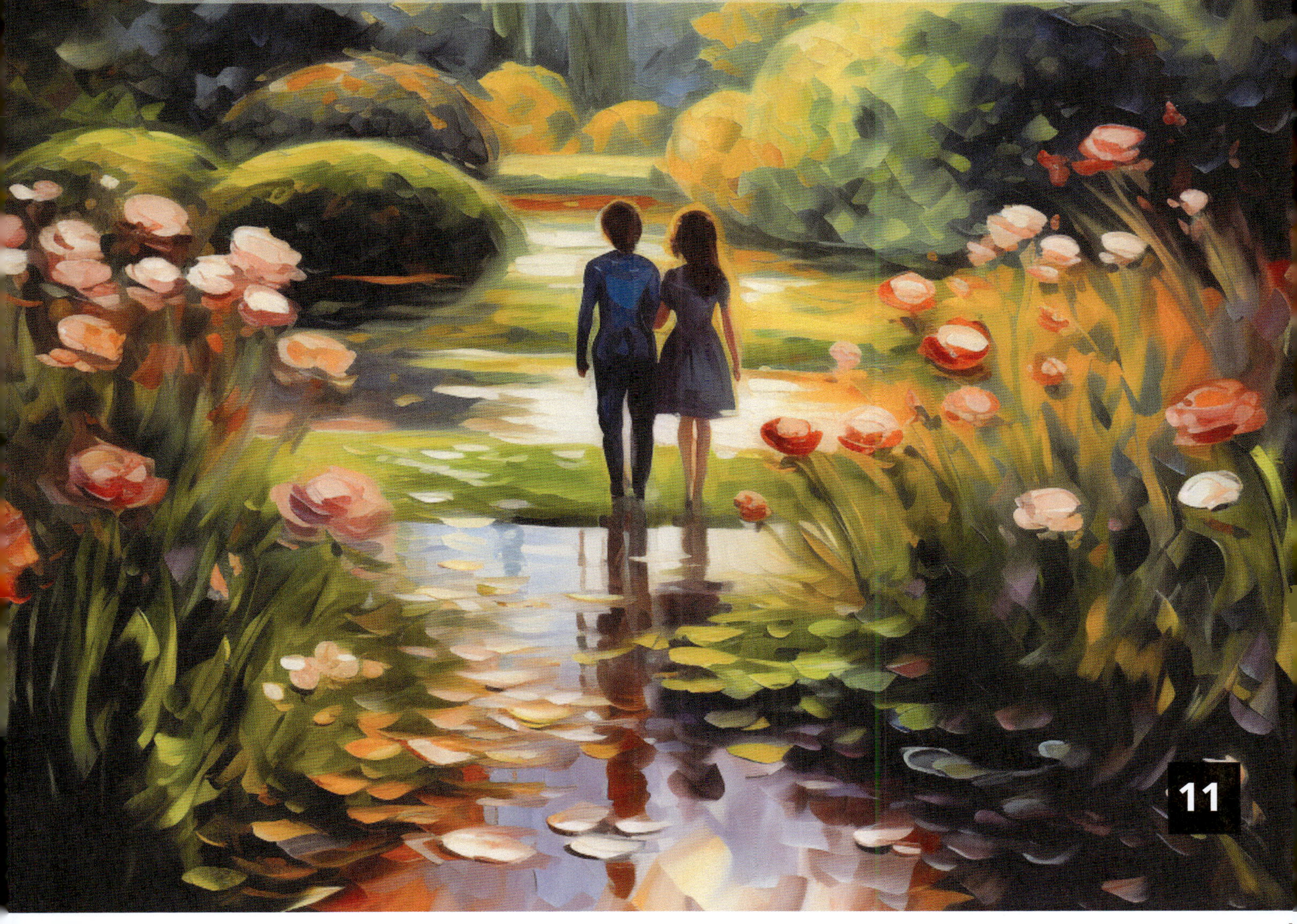

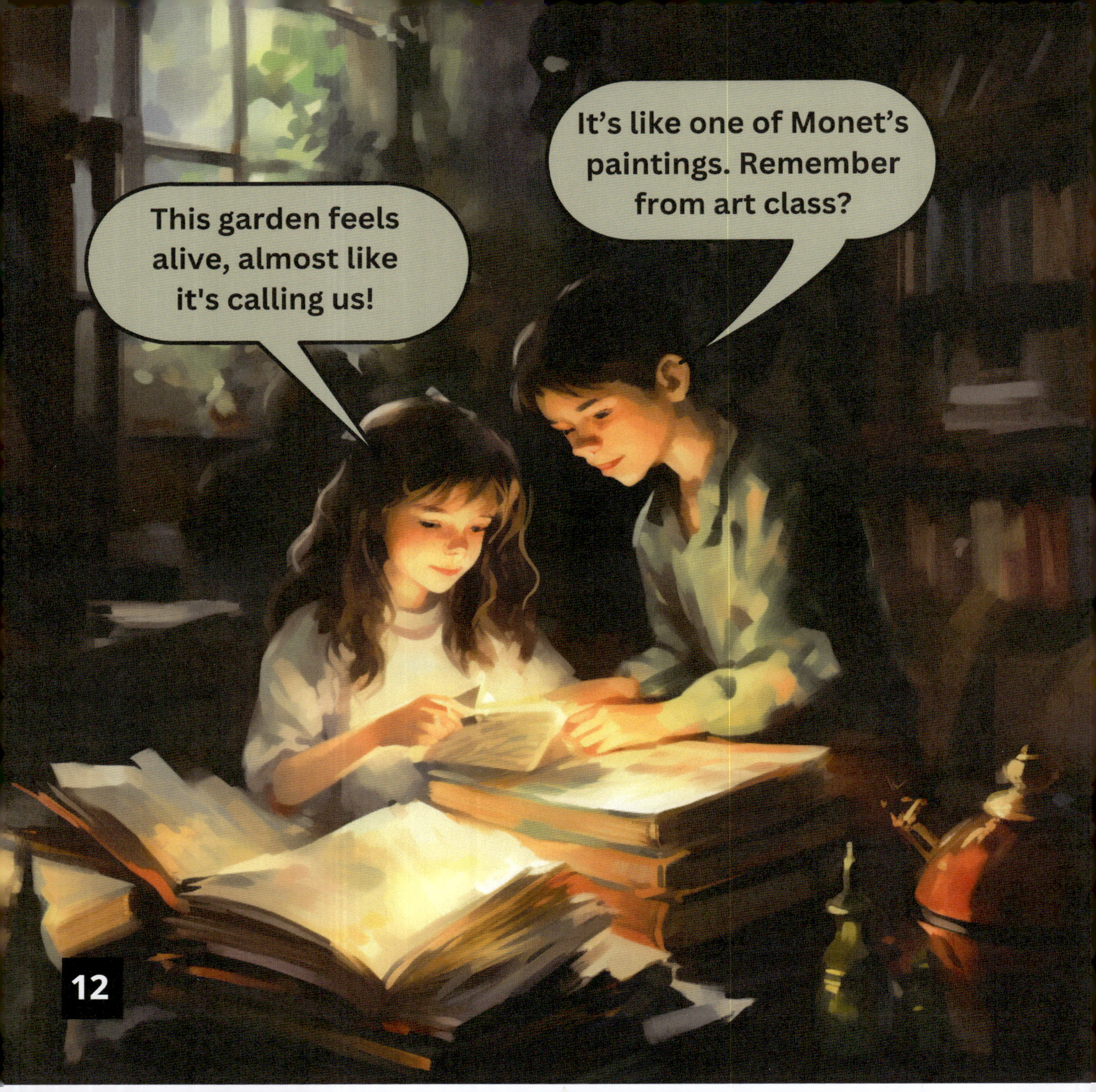
This garden feels alive, almost like it's calling us!
It's like one of Monet's paintings. Remember from art class?

Claude Monet, a painter bold and bright, loved gardens and light. He started Impressionism, making blurry and bright his artistic vision. His garden at Giverny was his pride, where nature and art collide.

Impressionism, emerging in France in the late 1800s, was a major art movement emphasizing the artist's perception of nature rather than exact representation. Characterized by distinctive brushwork and innovative use of light, it marked a departure from traditional art forms and laid the groundwork for modern painting.

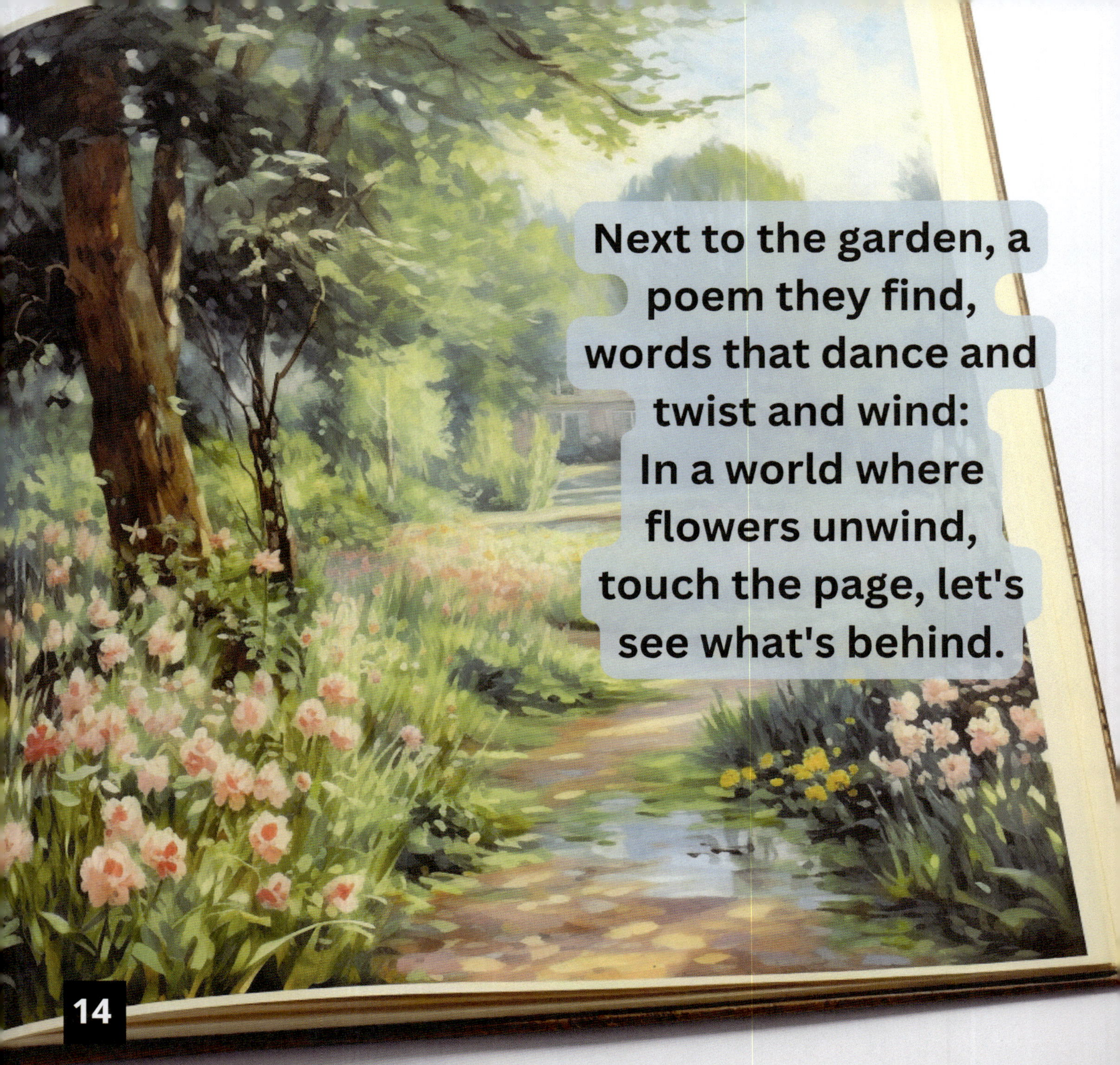

Next to the garden, a
poem they find,
words that dance and
twist and wind:
In a world where
flowers unwind,
touch the page, let's
see what's behind.

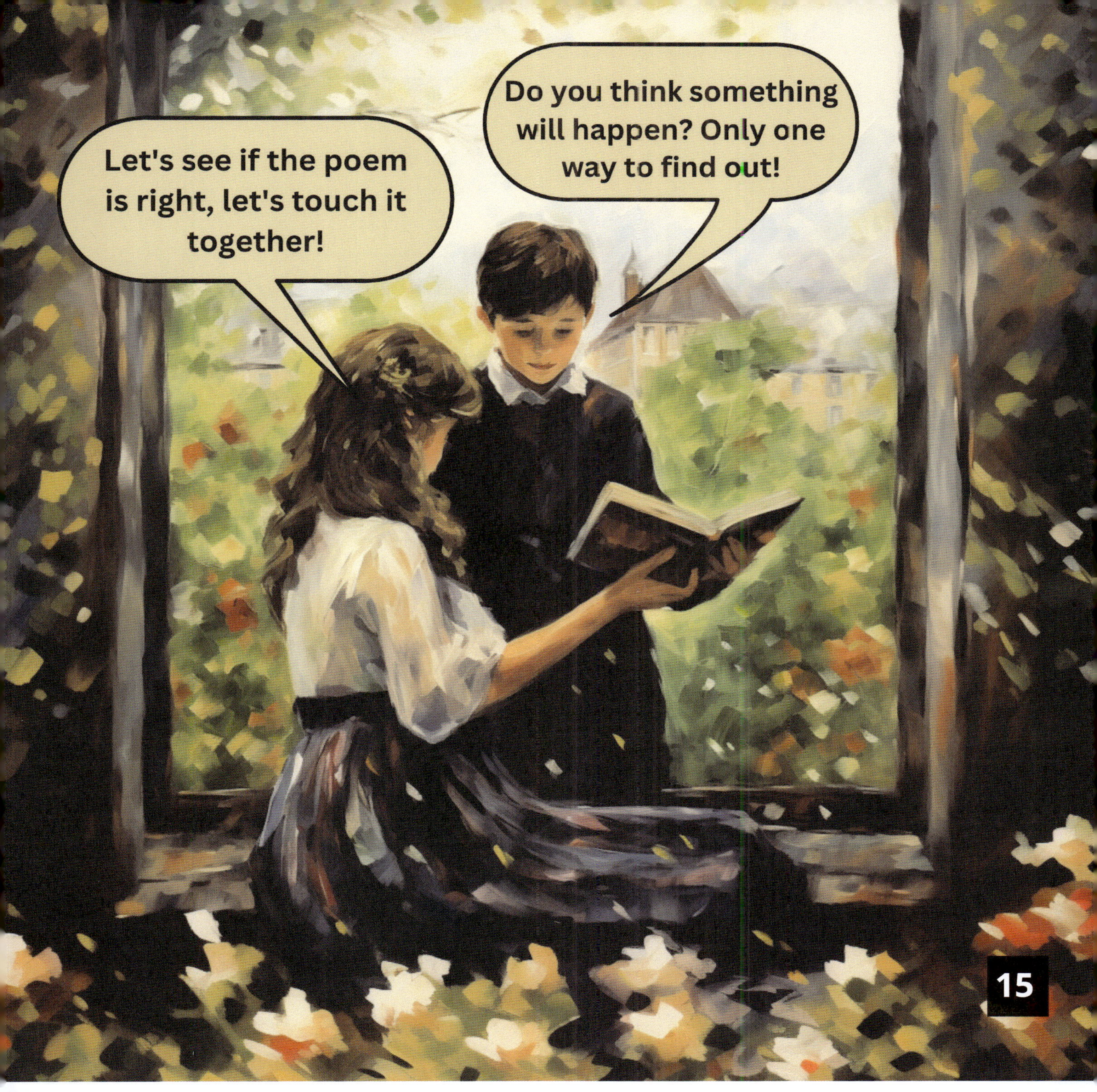
Let's see if the poem is right, let's touch it together!
Do you think something will happen? Only one way to find out!

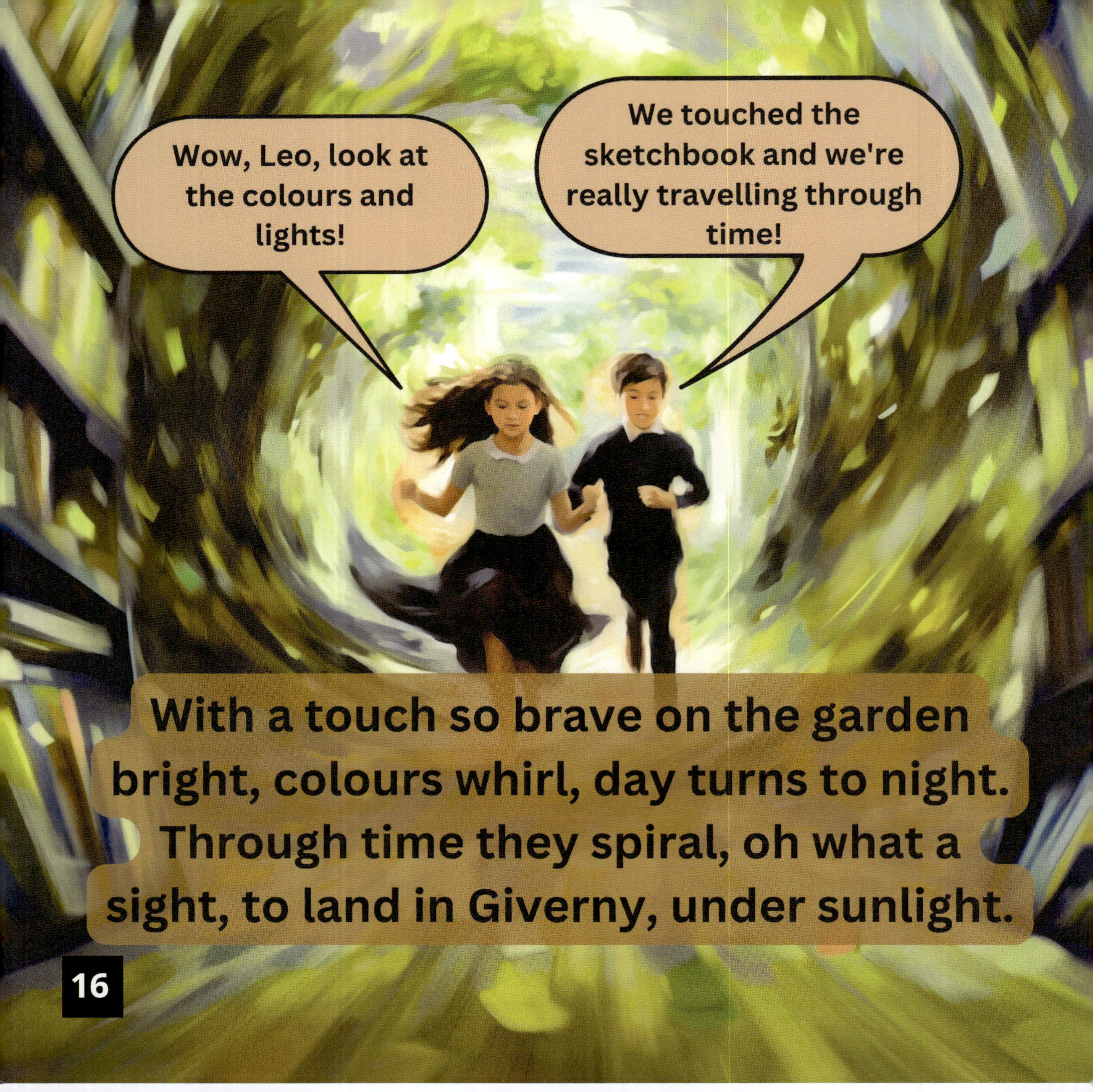

With a touch so brave on the garden bright, colours whirl, day turns to night. Through time they spiral, oh what a sight, to land in Giverny, under sunlight.

In a garden of dreams, where colours blend,
Emma and Leo find their journey's bend.
Giverny in bloom, beauty without end,
in Monet's world, time they spend.

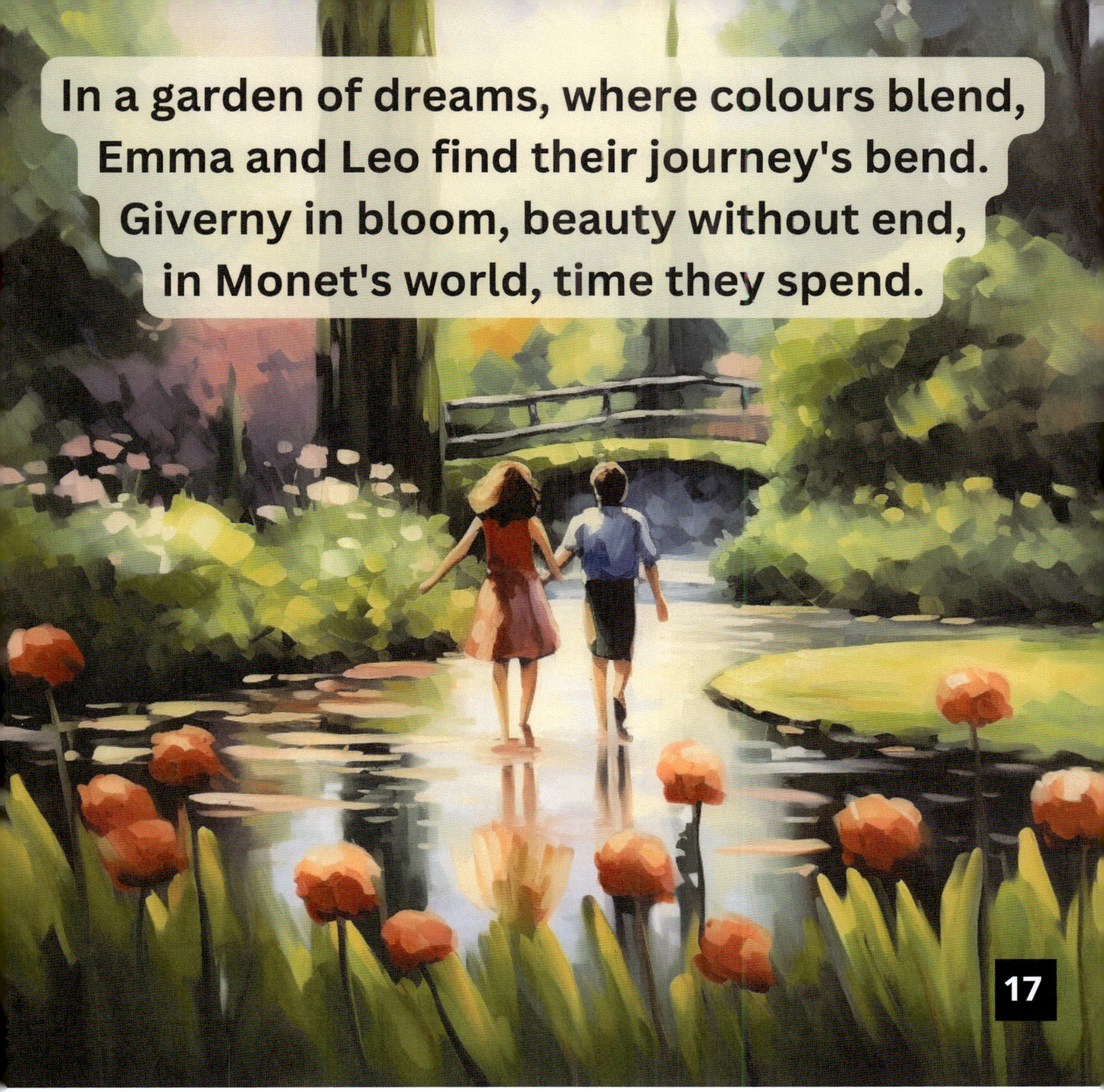

‘Look, Emma, see the artists' stance,
painting gardens, lost in trance. Just like
Monet, in time's romance, we've
travelled back, in art's expanse.’

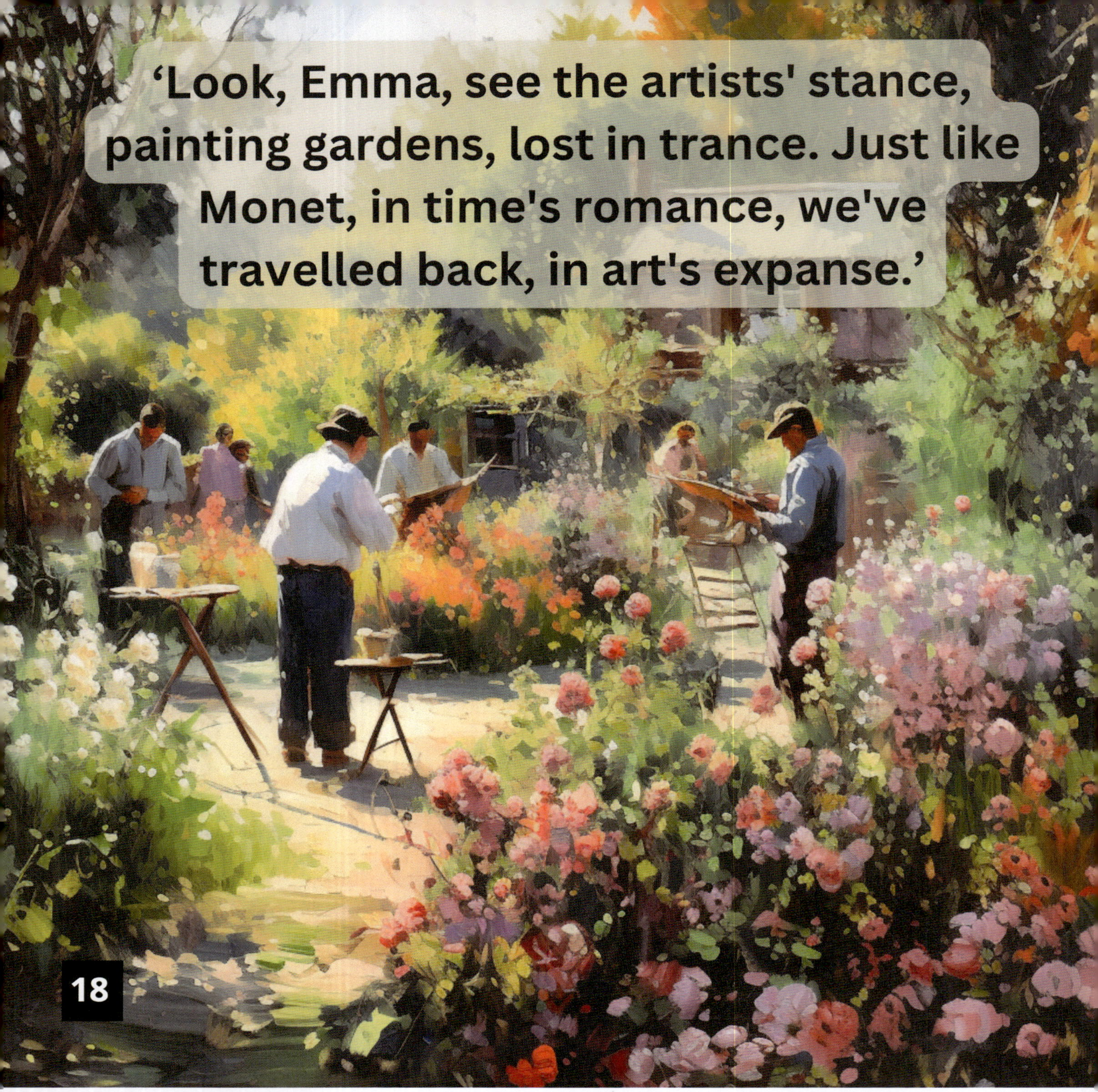

Now it's your turn, in this tale so grand,
draw your garden, let your imagination land.
Will it have flowers, trees, or something more?
Create your garden, open the door.
"

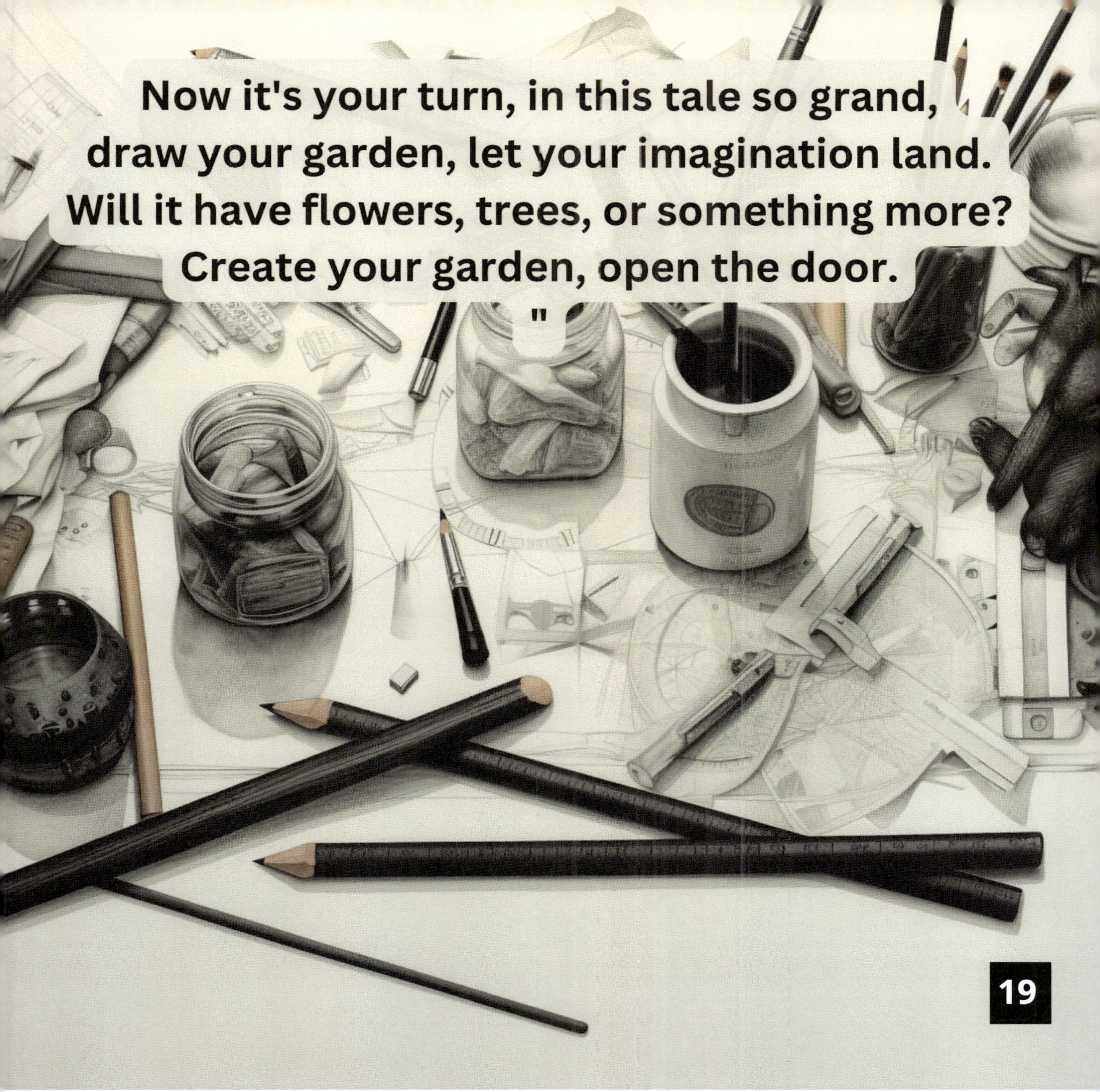

Activity: Space for you to draw your favourite garden.

Next page activity: Spot the Difference: Compare two seemingly identical images of Monet's studio and find the 4 subtle differences.

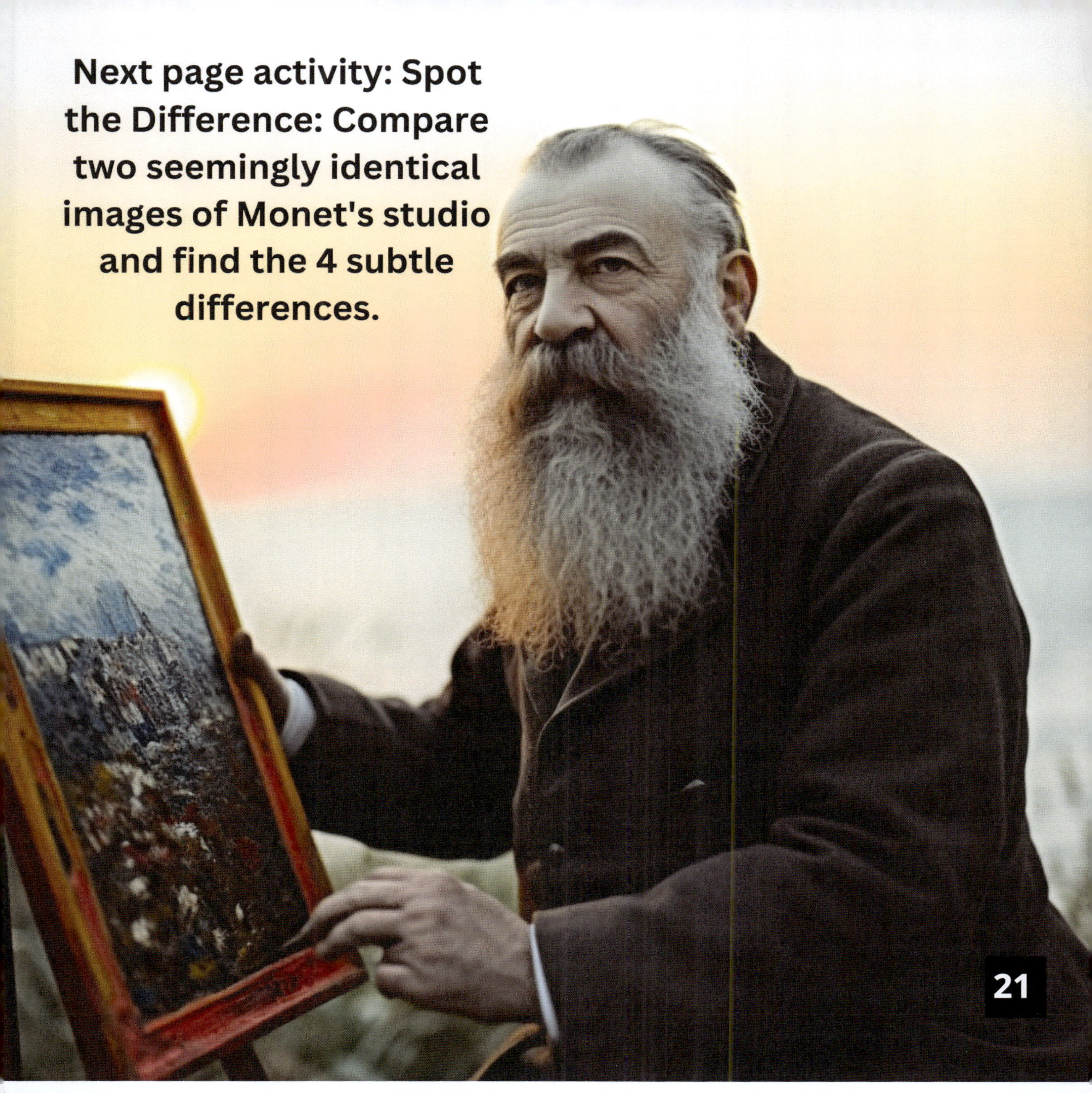

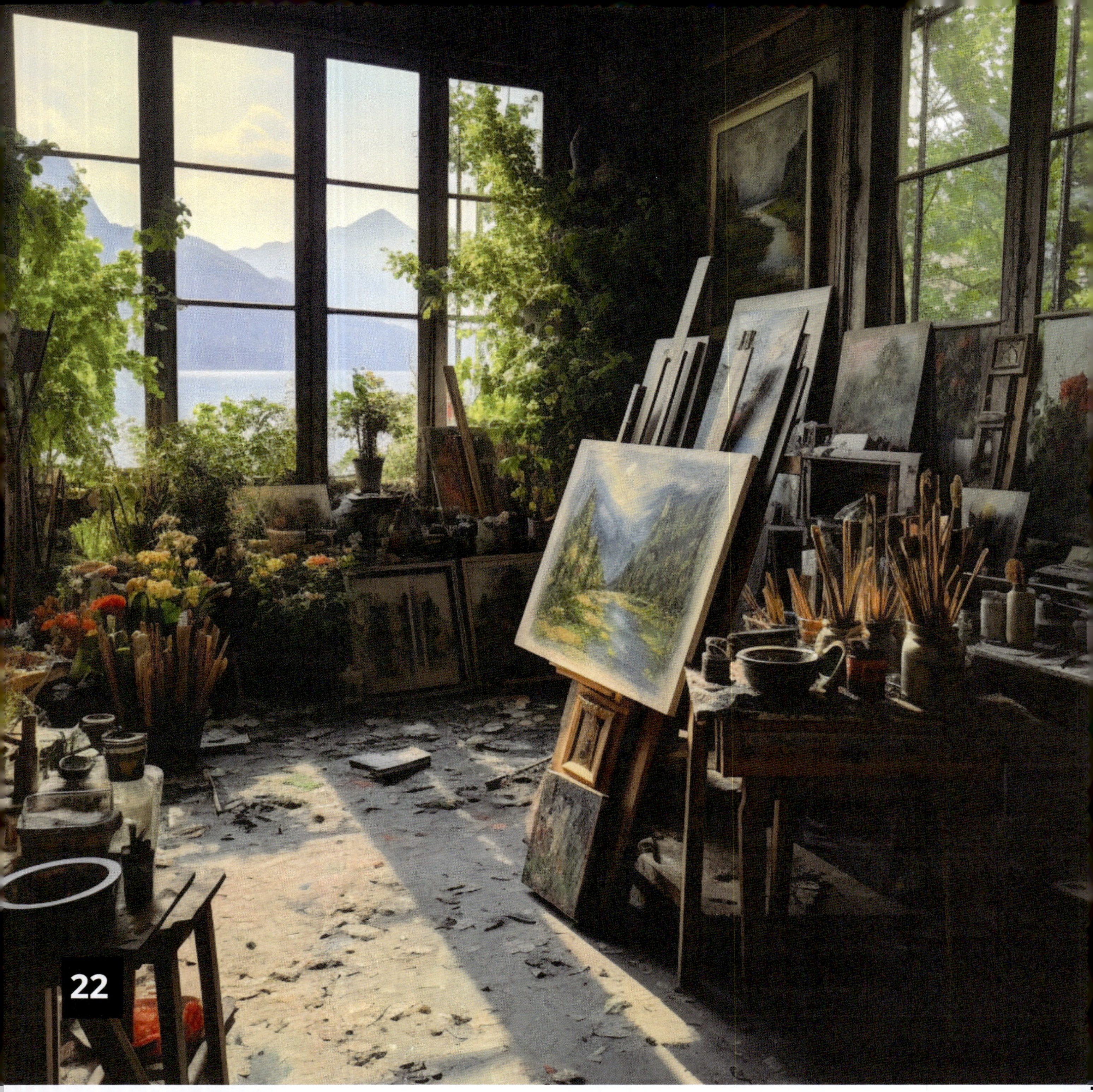

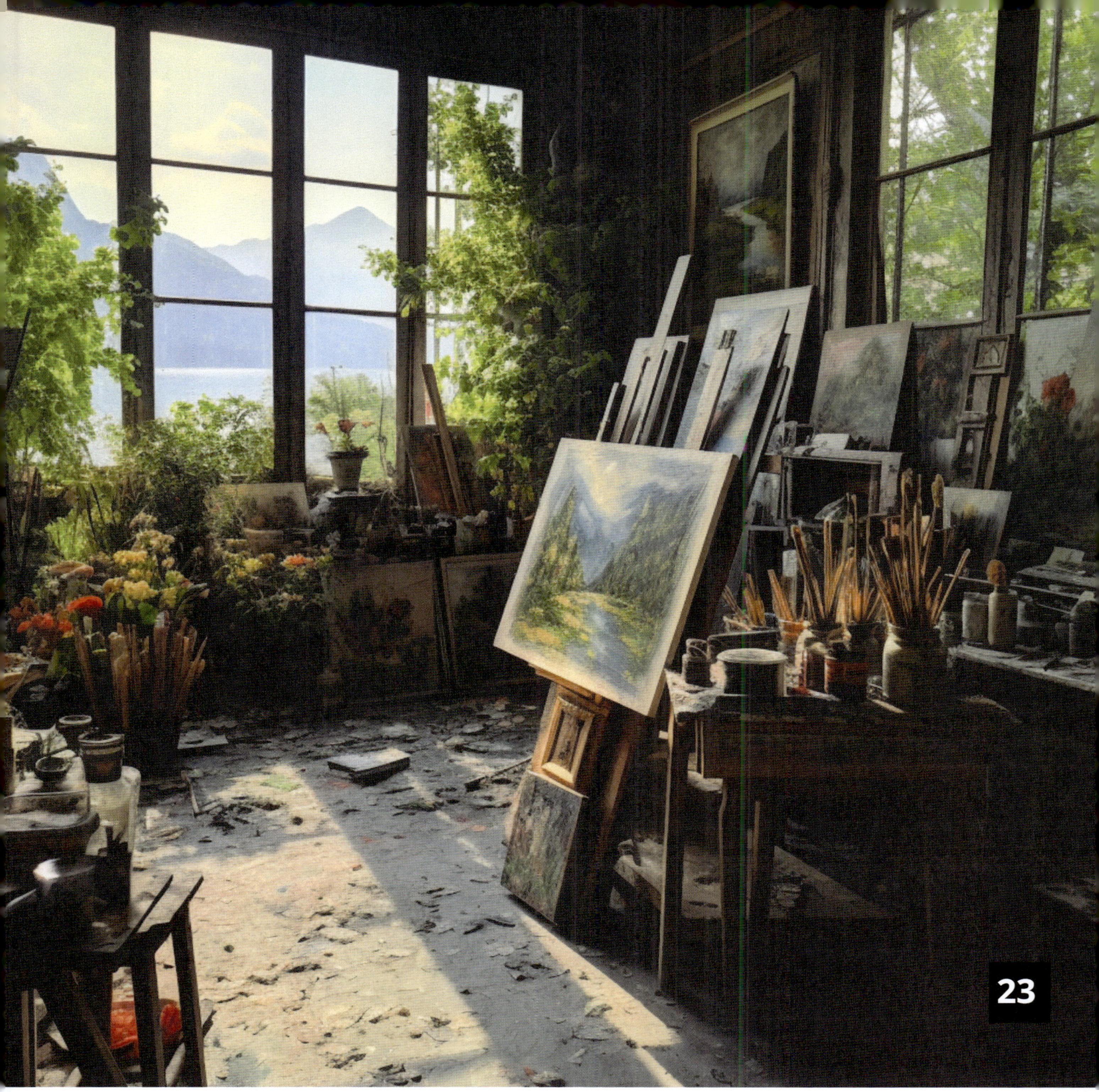

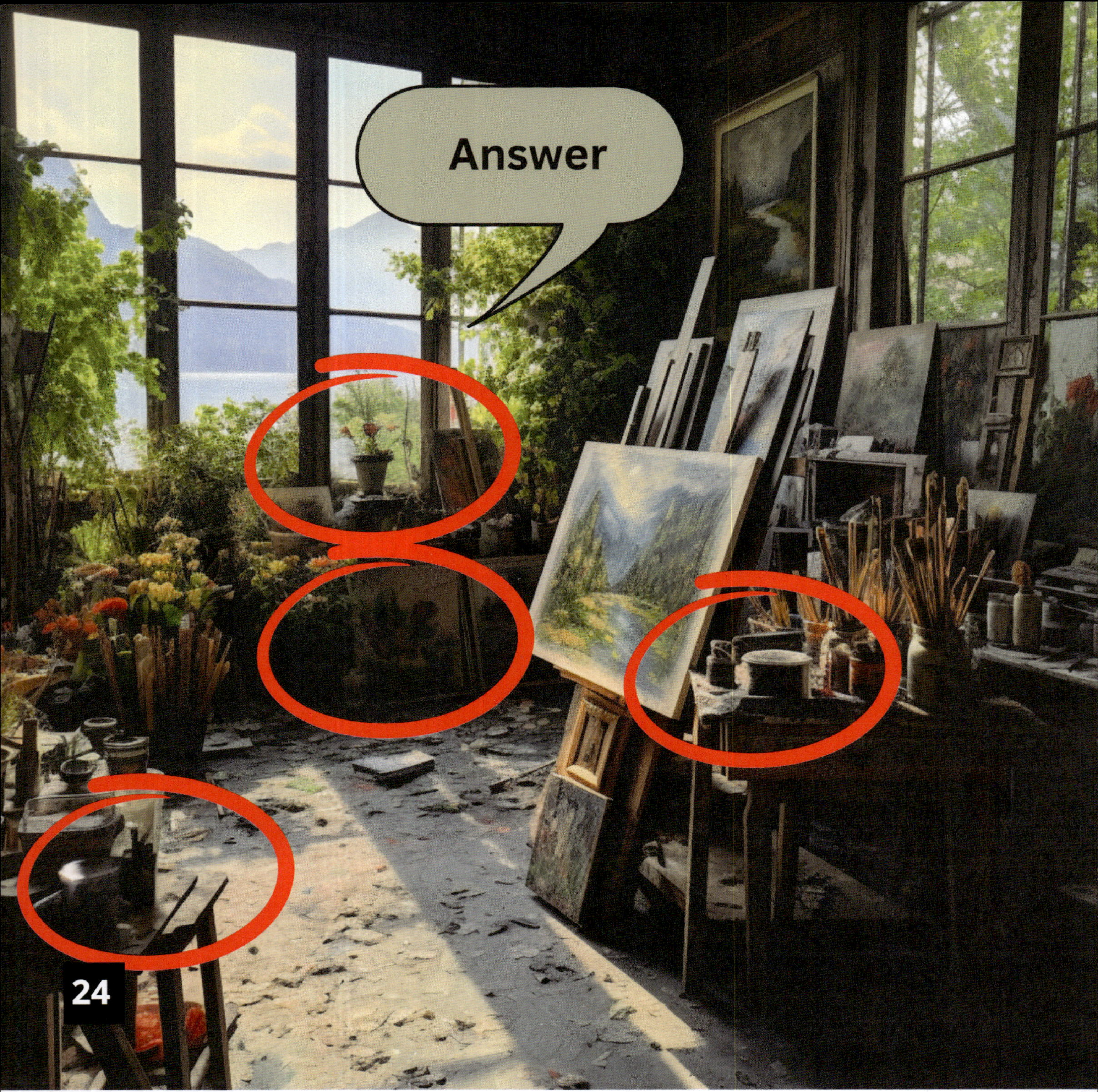
Answer

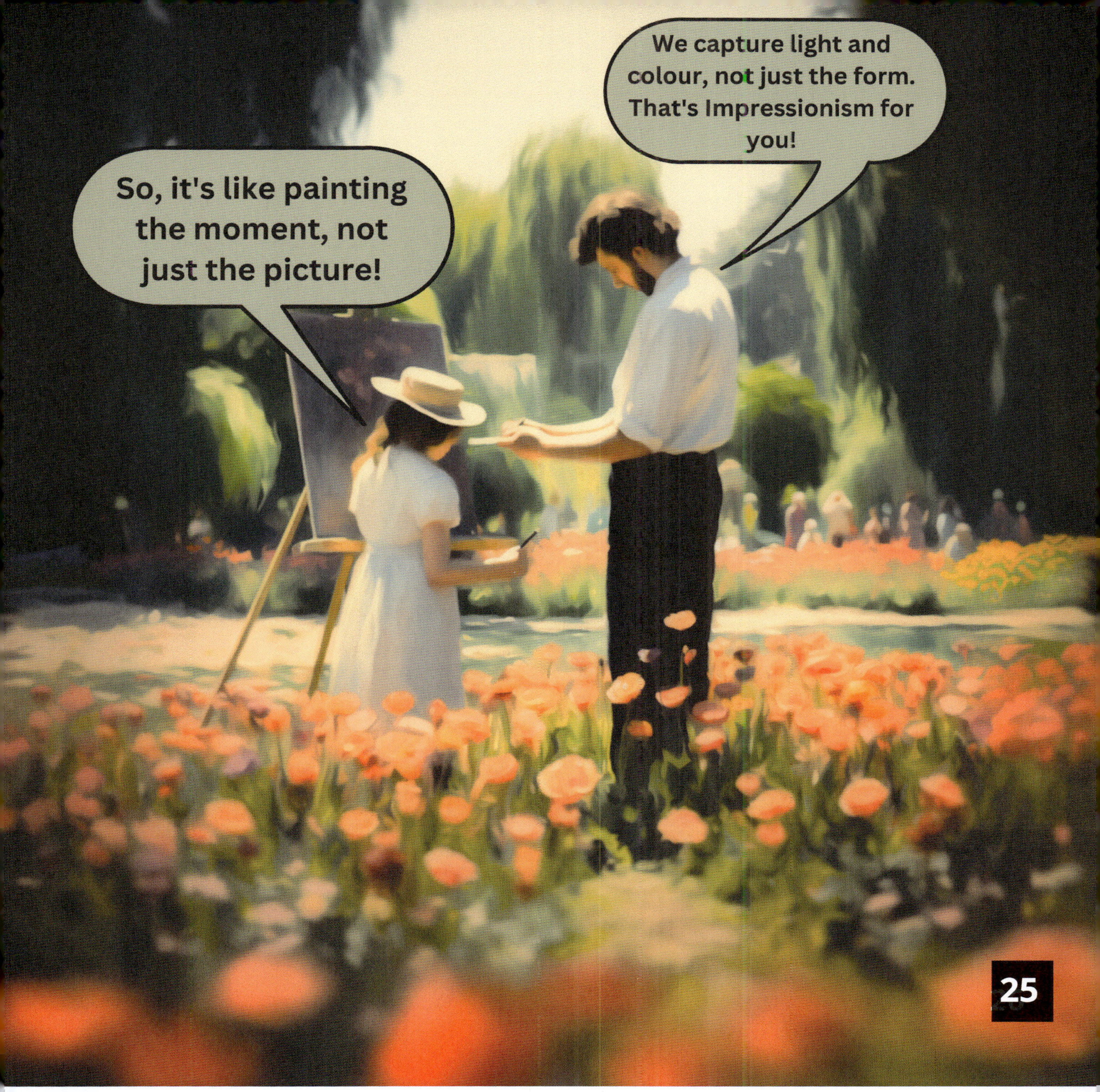
We capture light and colour, not just the form. That's Impressionism for you!
So, it's like painting the moment, not just the picture!

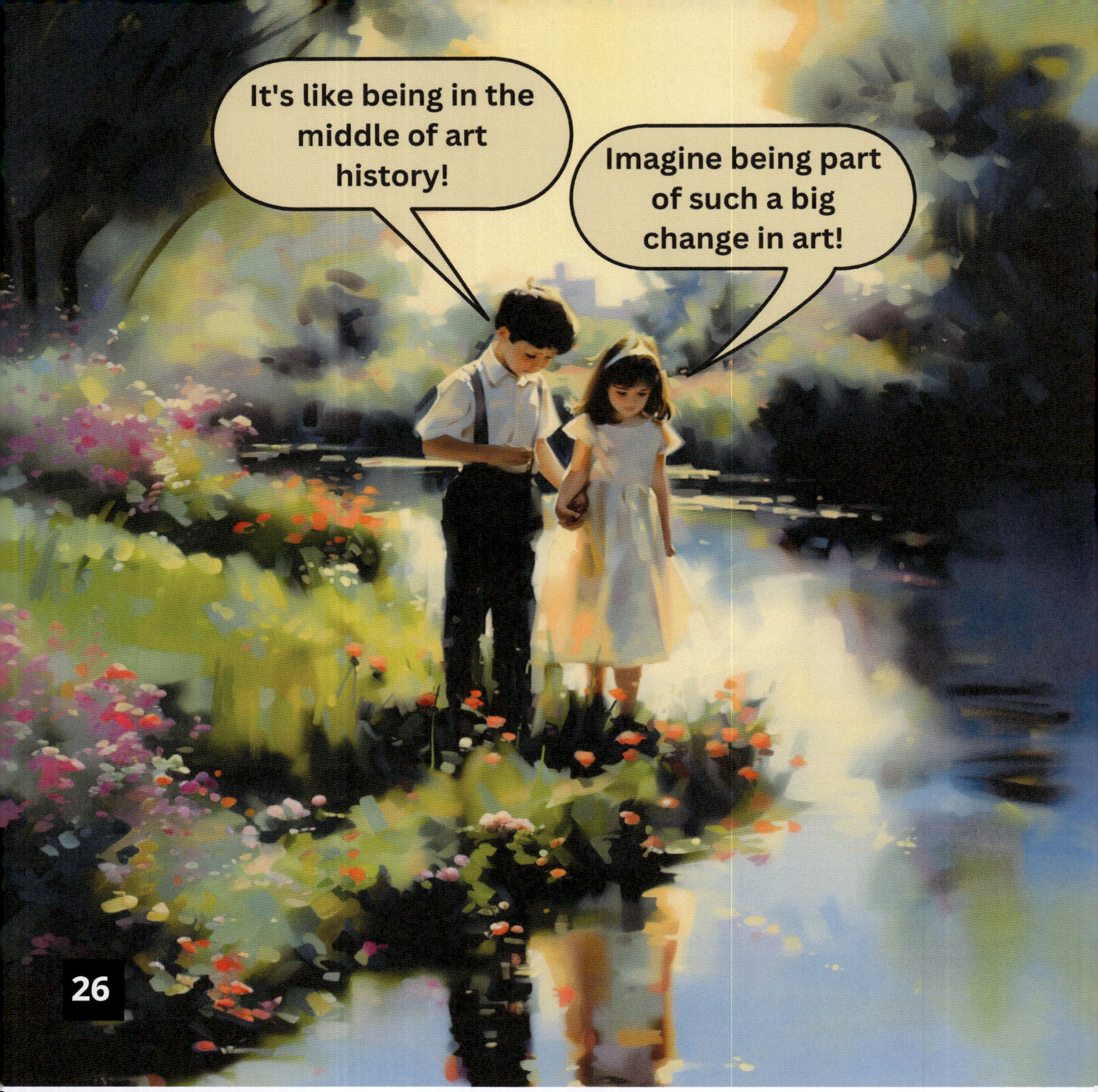
It's like being in the middle of art history!
Imagine being part of such a big change in art!

By the pond where the Lilies float and sway, Emma and Leo dream away. If through art, you could travel any day, where would you go, what would you say?

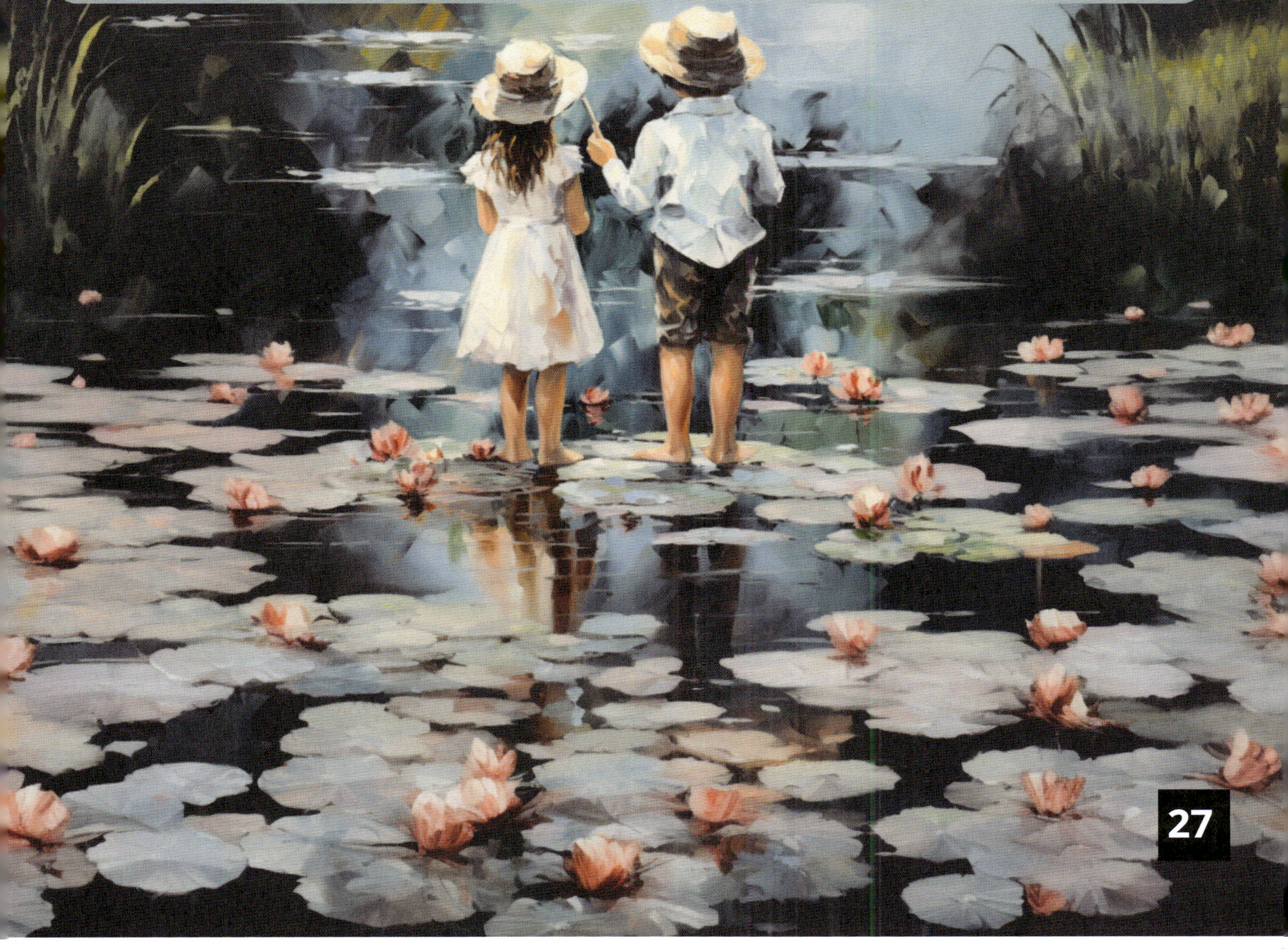

Activity: Space for you to write or draw where you would go if could travel through art.

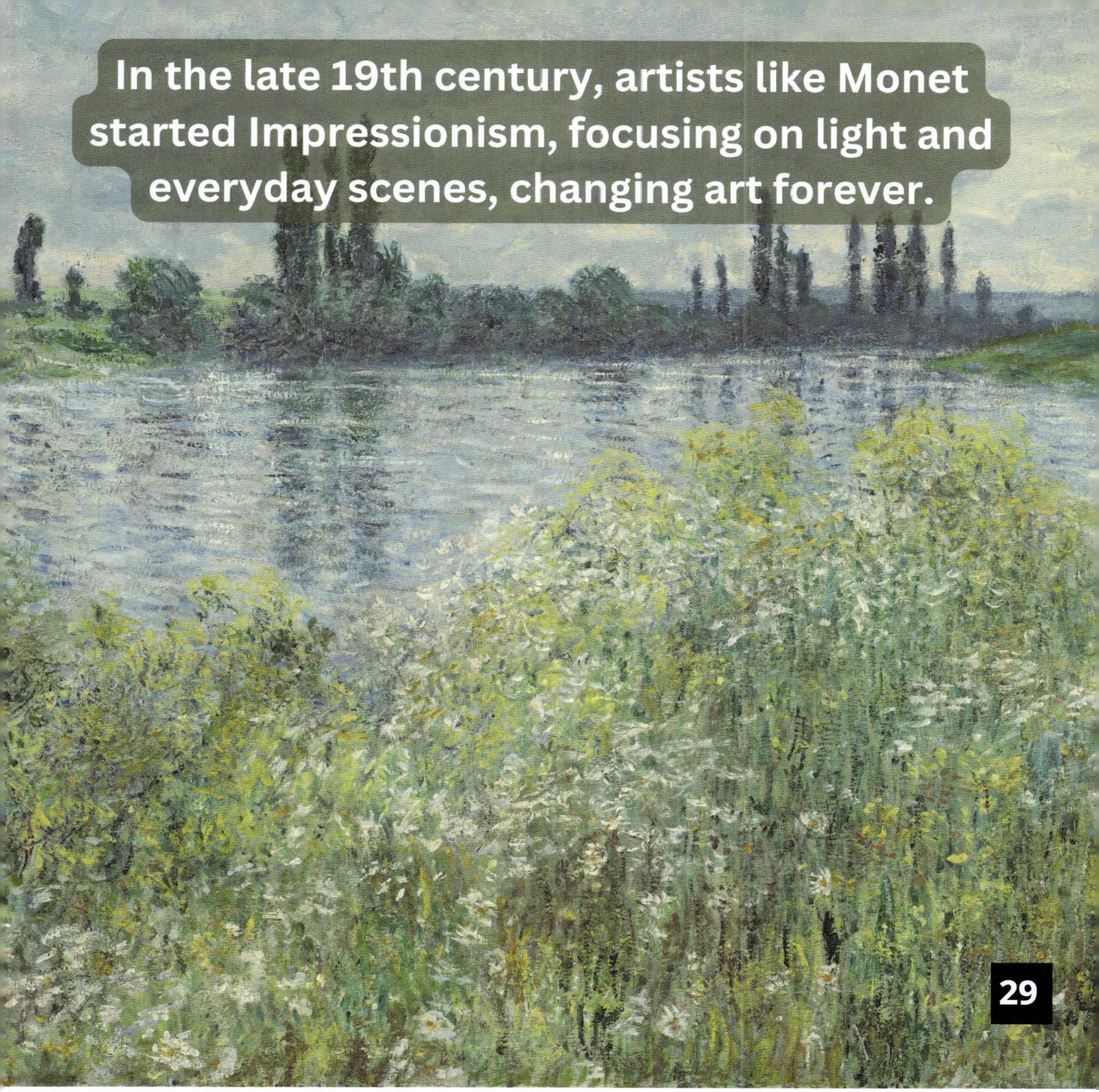

In the late 19th century, artists like Monet started Impressionism, focusing on light and everyday scenes, changing art forever.

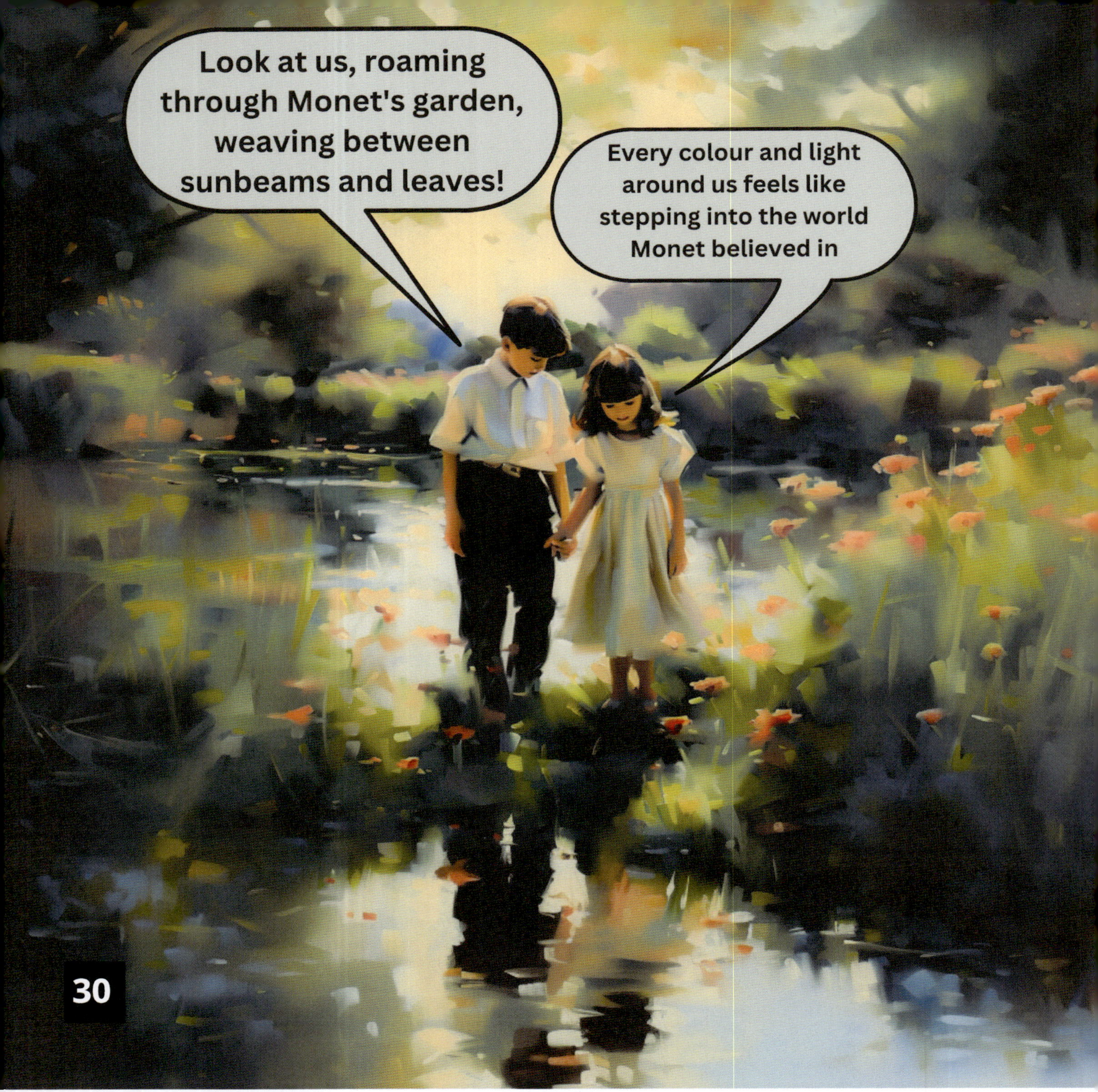
Look at us, roaming through Monet's garden, weaving between sunbeams and leaves!
Every colour and light around us feels like stepping into the world Monet believed in

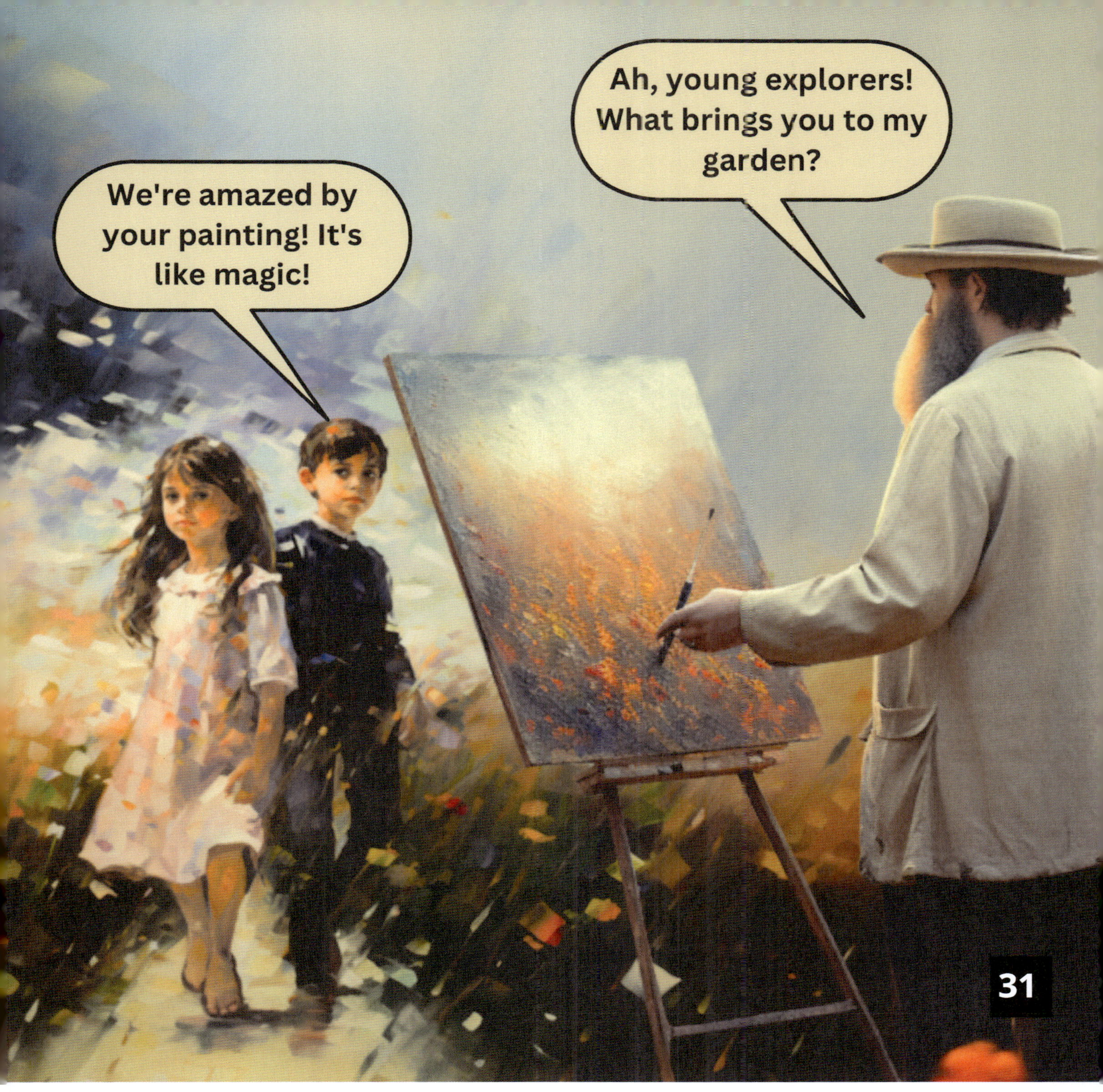
Ah, young explorers! What brings you to my garden?
We're amazed by your painting! It's like magic!

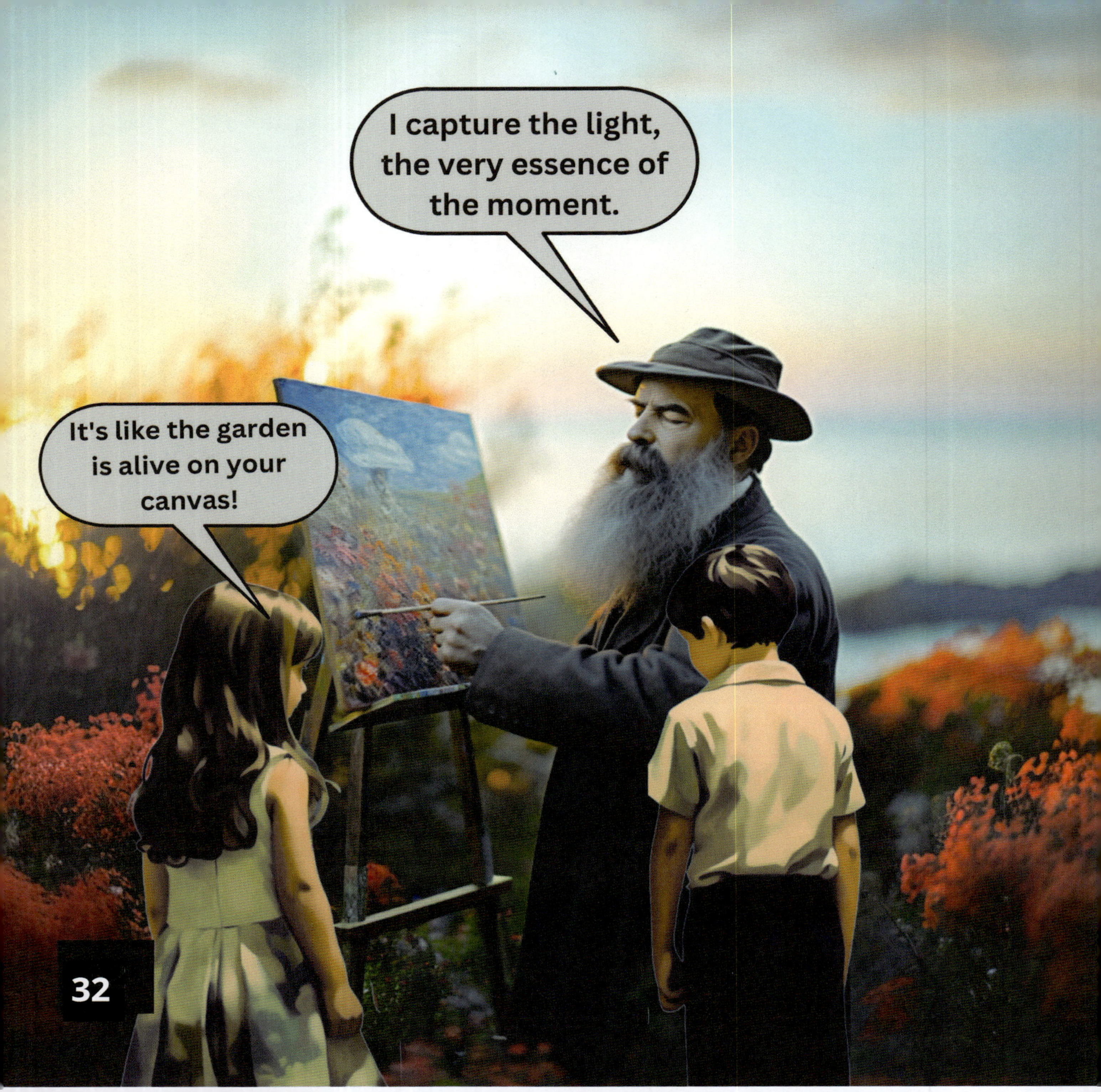
I capture the light, the very essence of the moment.
It's like the garden is alive on your canvas!

Monet's Impressionism: Painting not just what you see, but how you see it – with light, colour and quick brushstrokes.

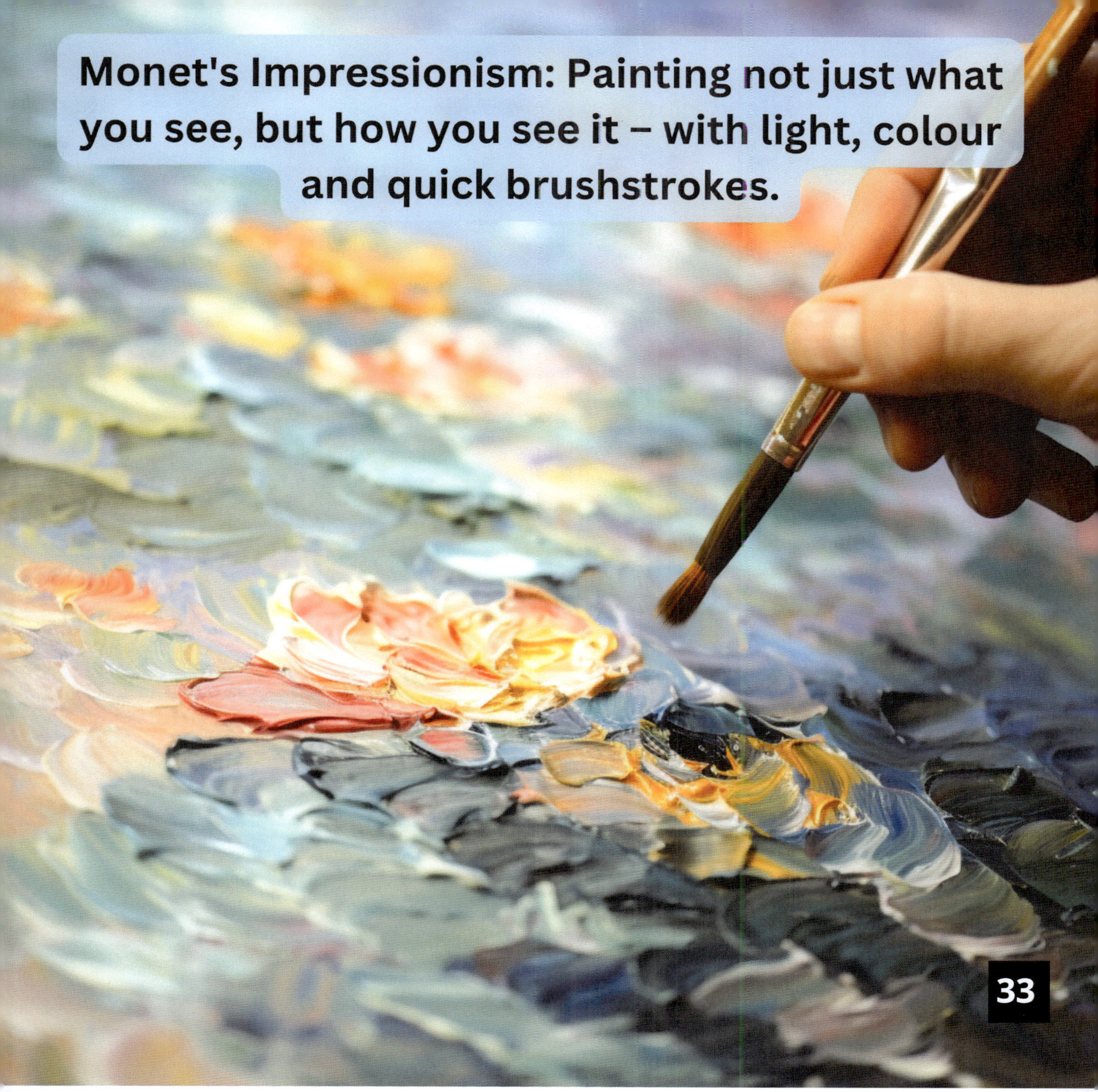

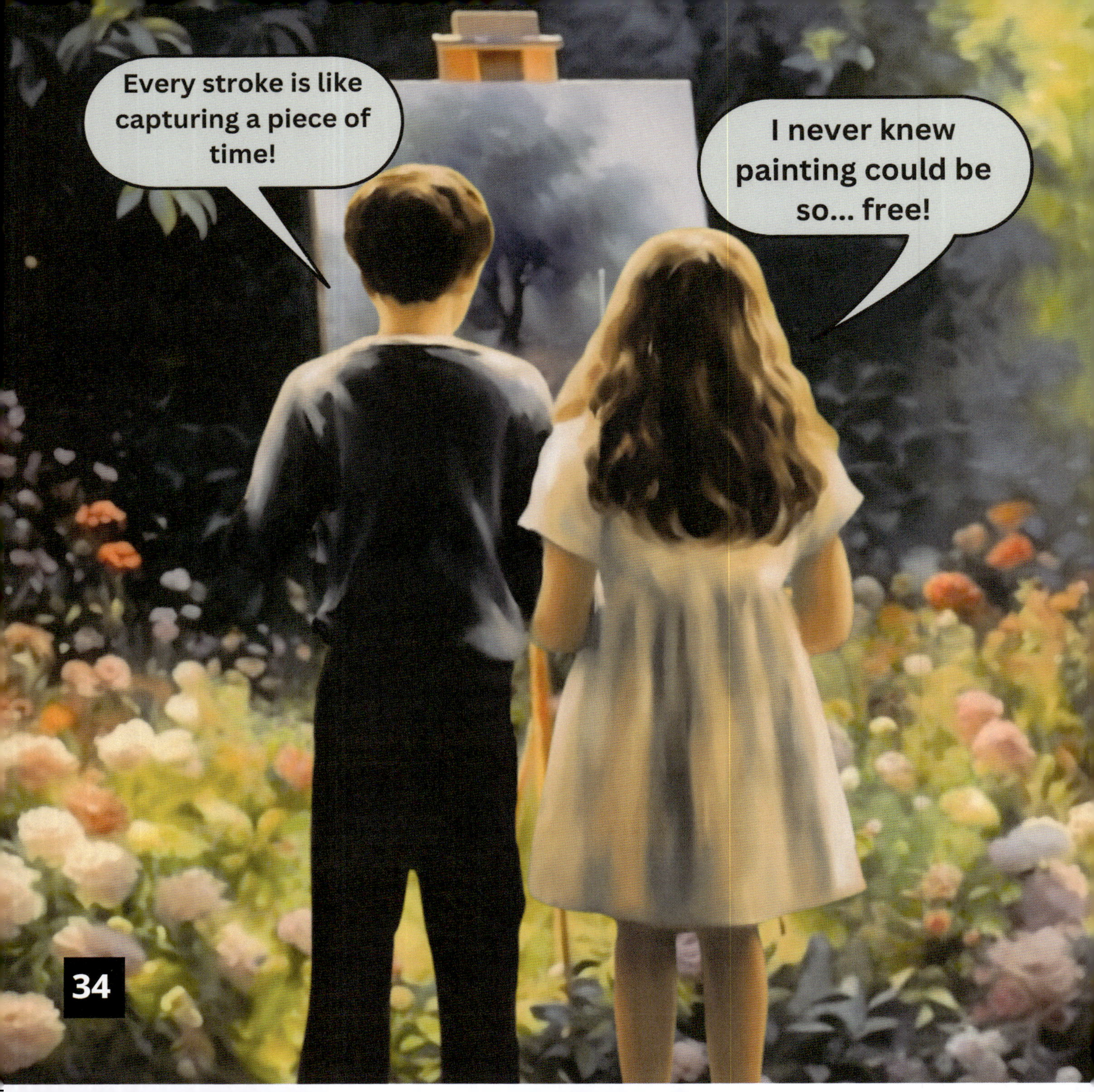
Every stroke is like capturing a piece of time!
I never knew painting could be so... free!

Two paintings alike, yet subtly apart, spot the 4 differences, use your heart. In each brushstroke, in each art. Find the changes, that's where you start.

Activity: Spot the Difference: Two similar paintings with 4 minor variations for you to identify.

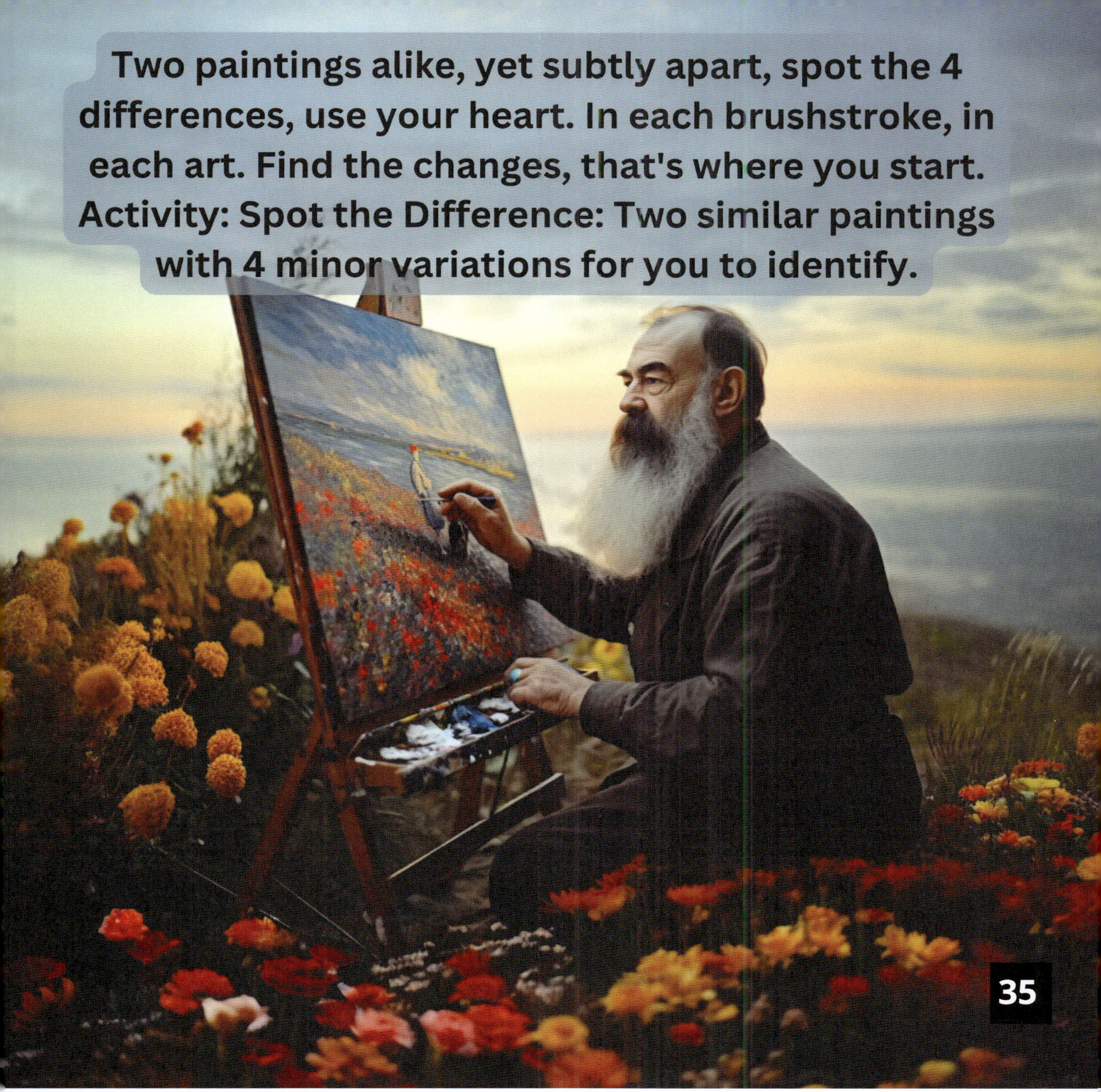

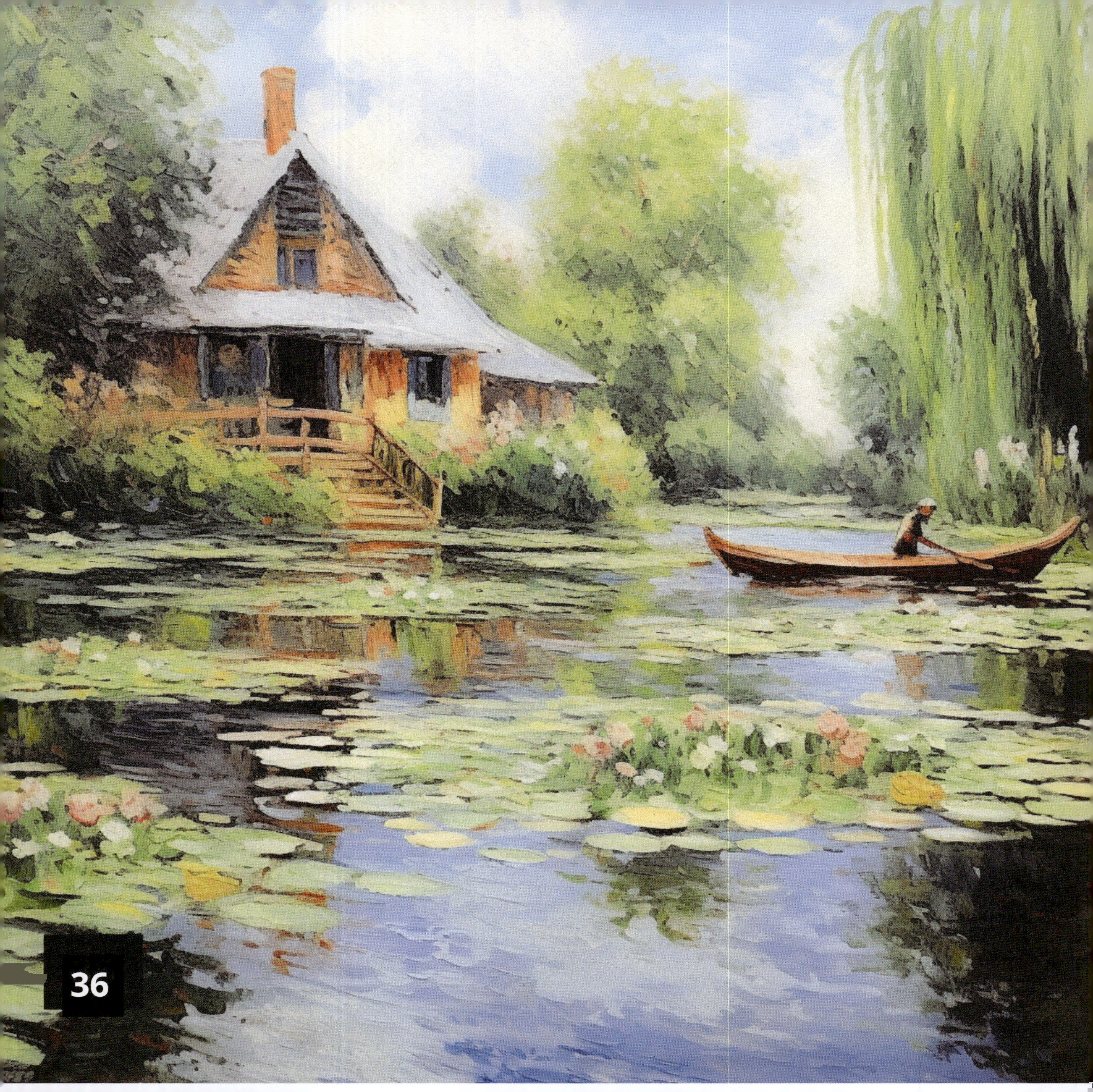

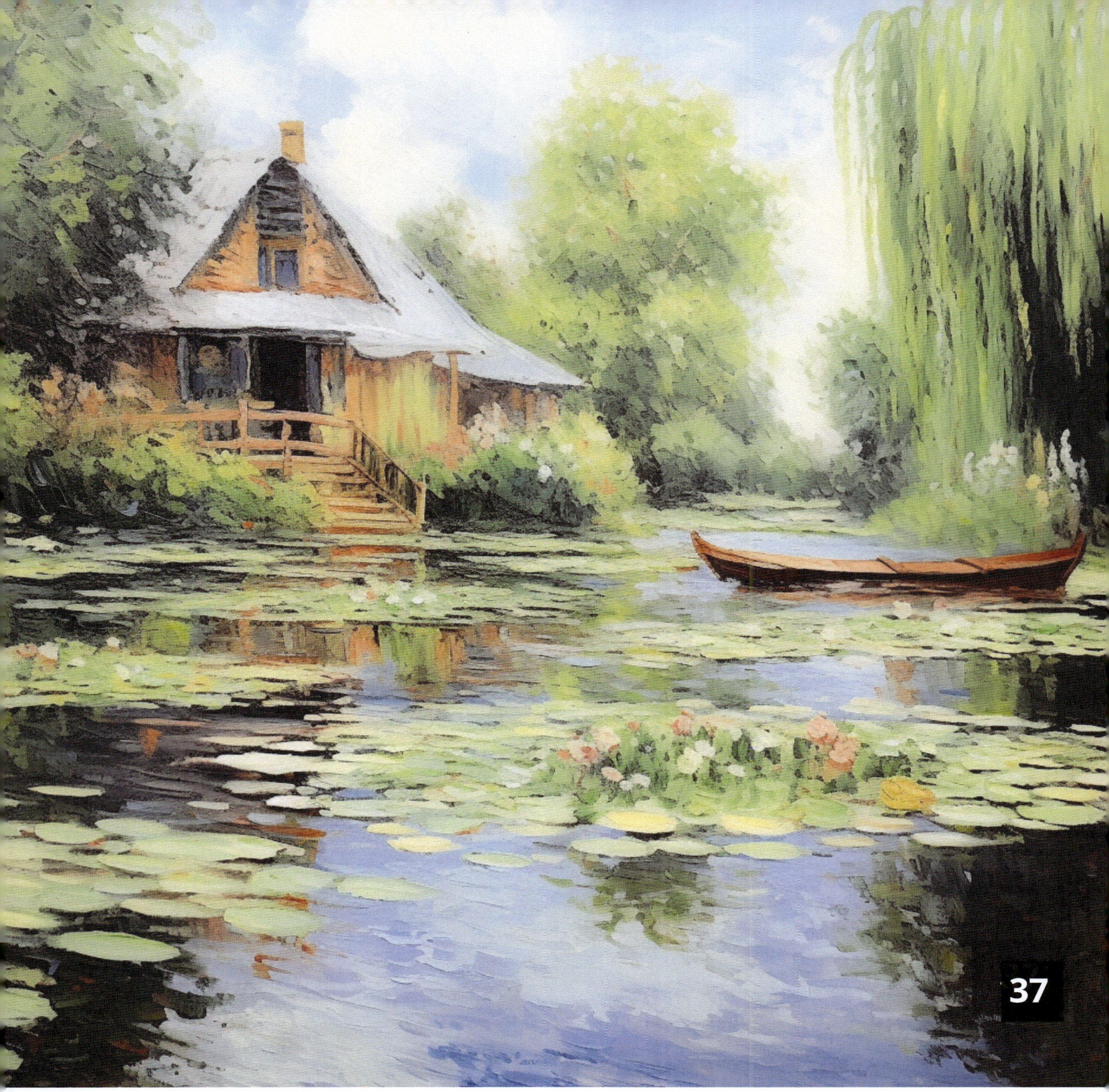

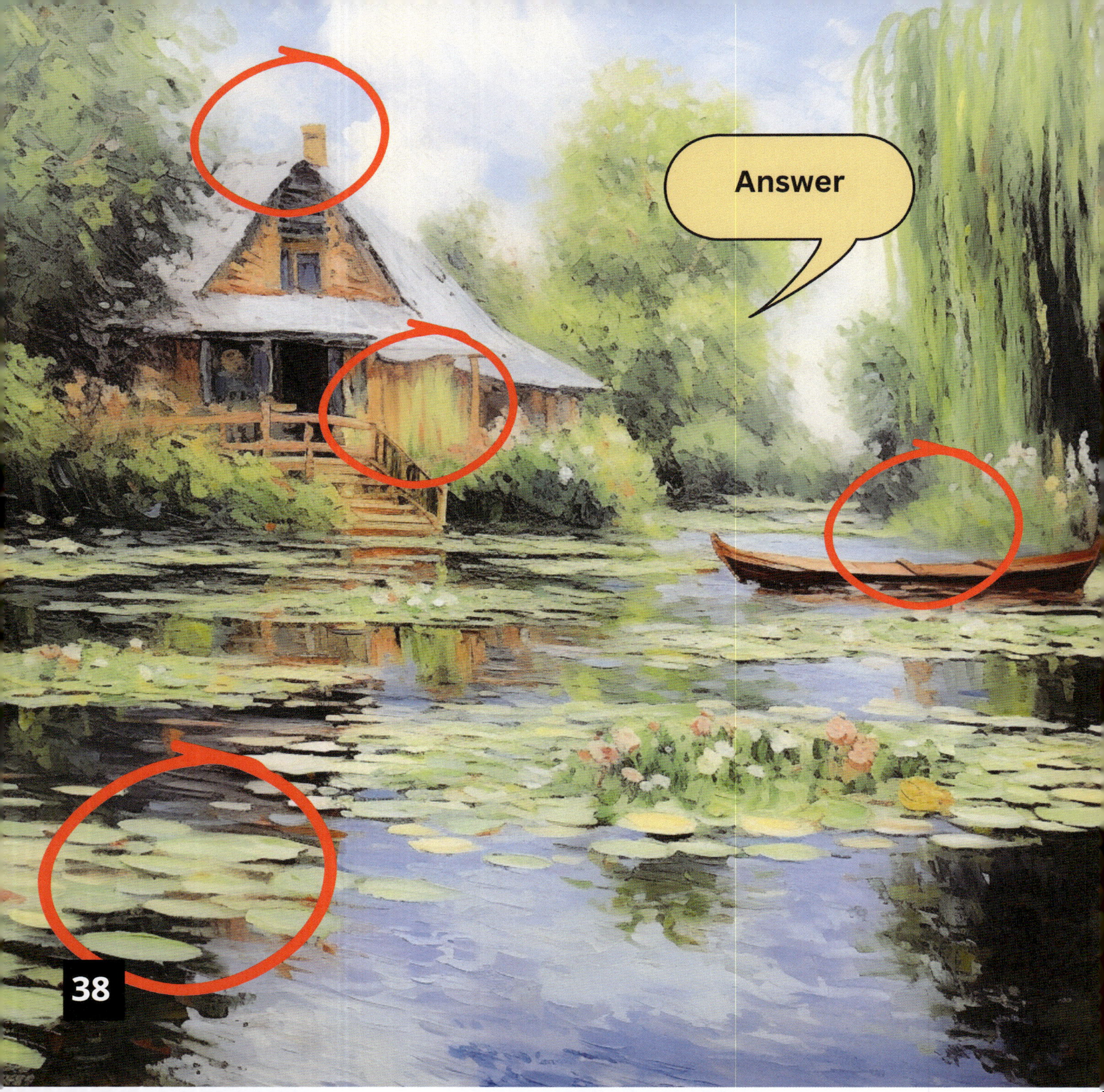
Answer

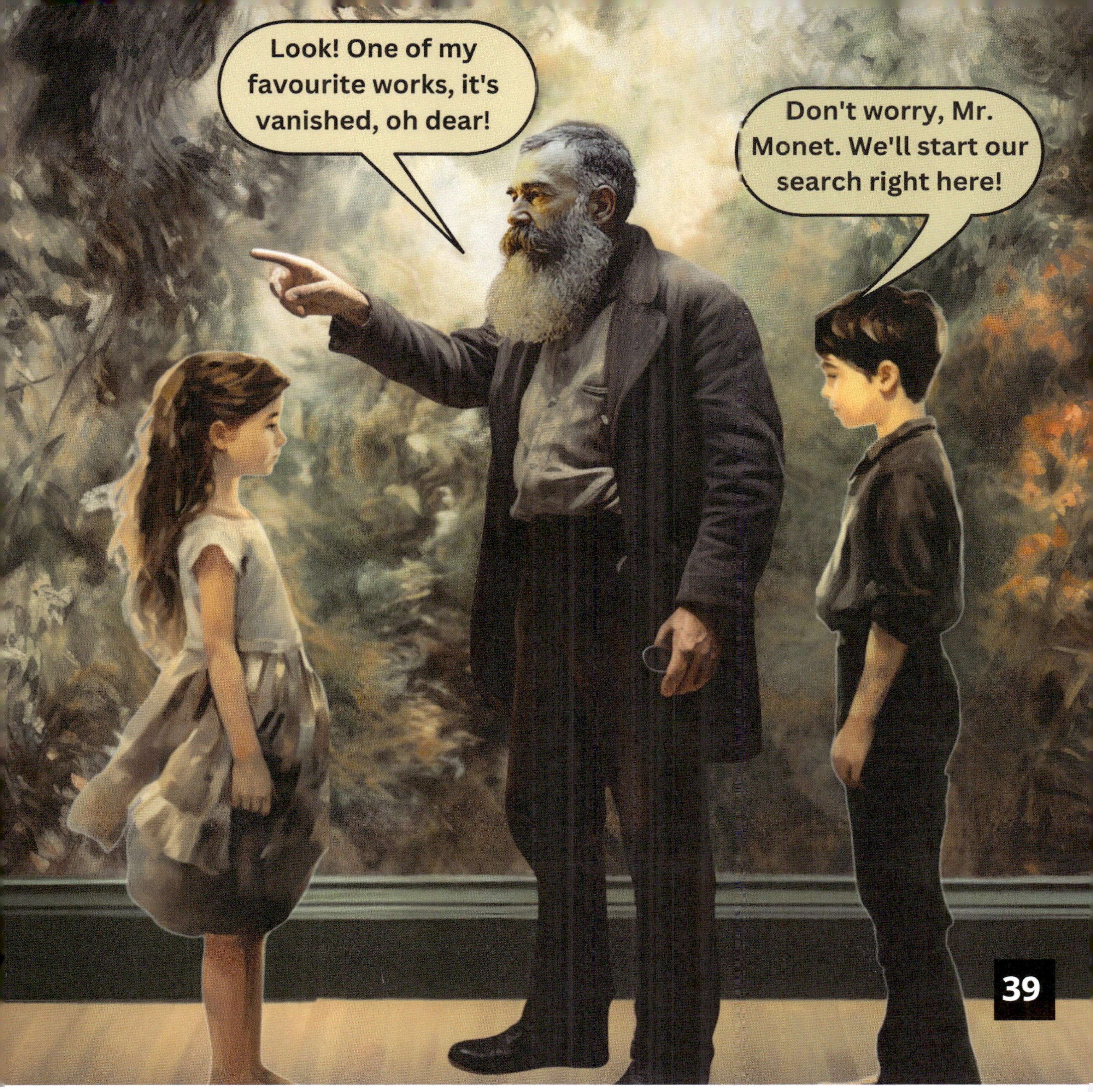
Look! One of my favourite works, it's vanished, oh dear!
Don't worry, Mr. Monet. We'll start our search right here!

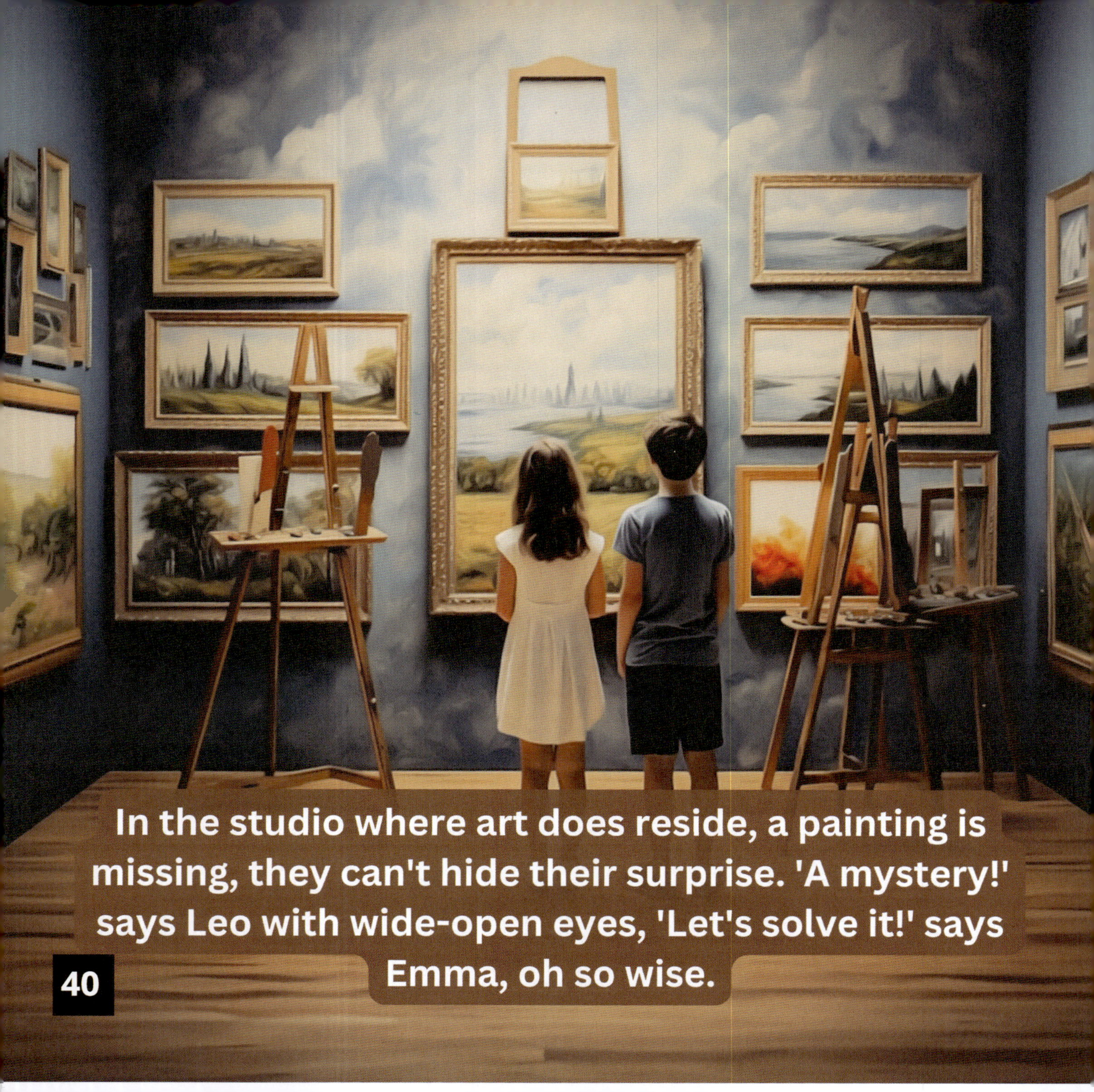

In the studio where art does reside, a painting is missing, they can't hide their surprise. 'A mystery!' says Leo with wide-open eyes, 'Let's solve it!' says Emma, oh so wise.

As they looked around, they observed Monet's style: a dance of light and color. His famous works, such as "The Artist's Garden in Argenteuil," reflect Monet's fascination with the interplay of light, color, and nature, capturing a vibrant scene of his garden in full bloom.

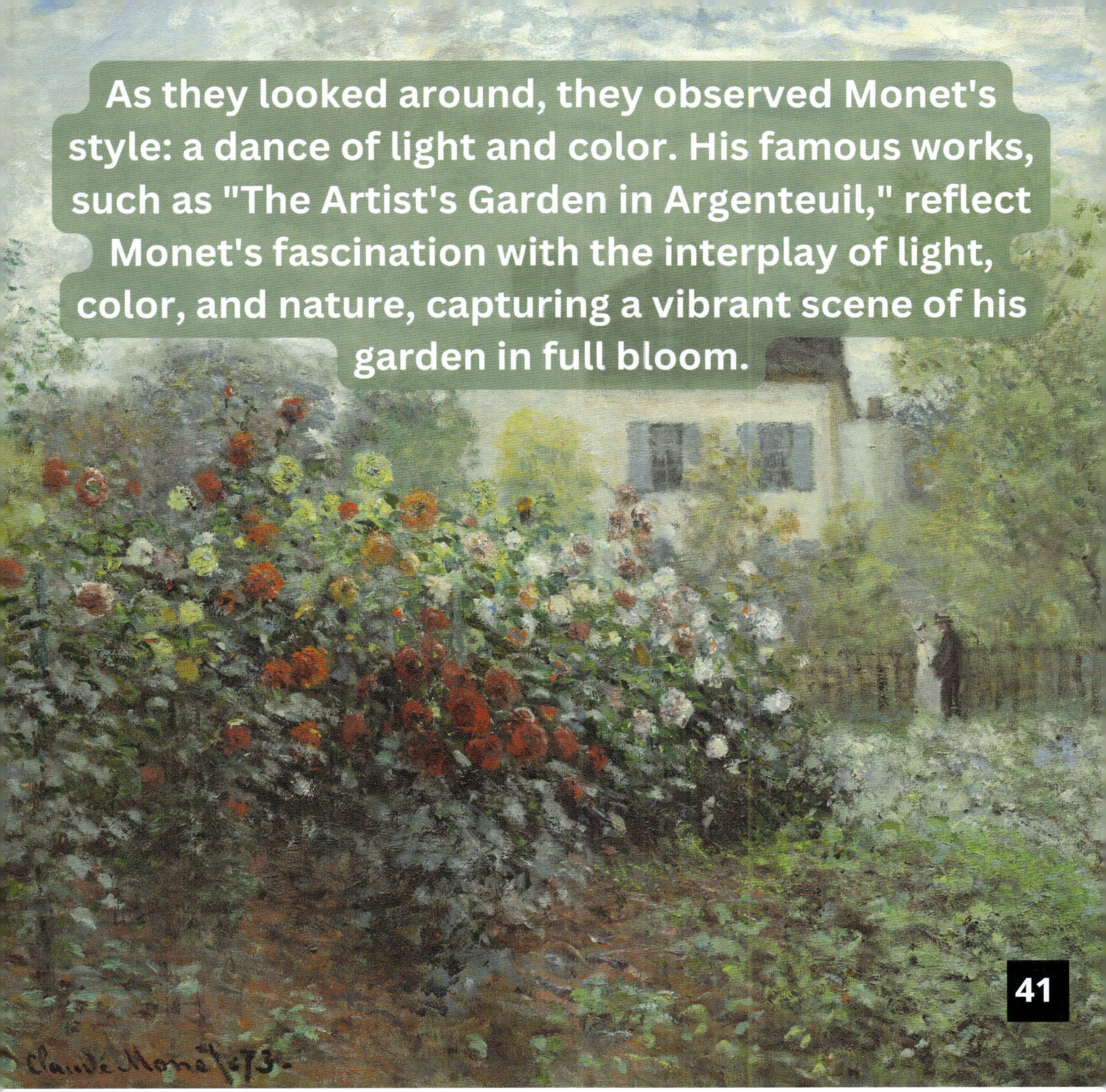

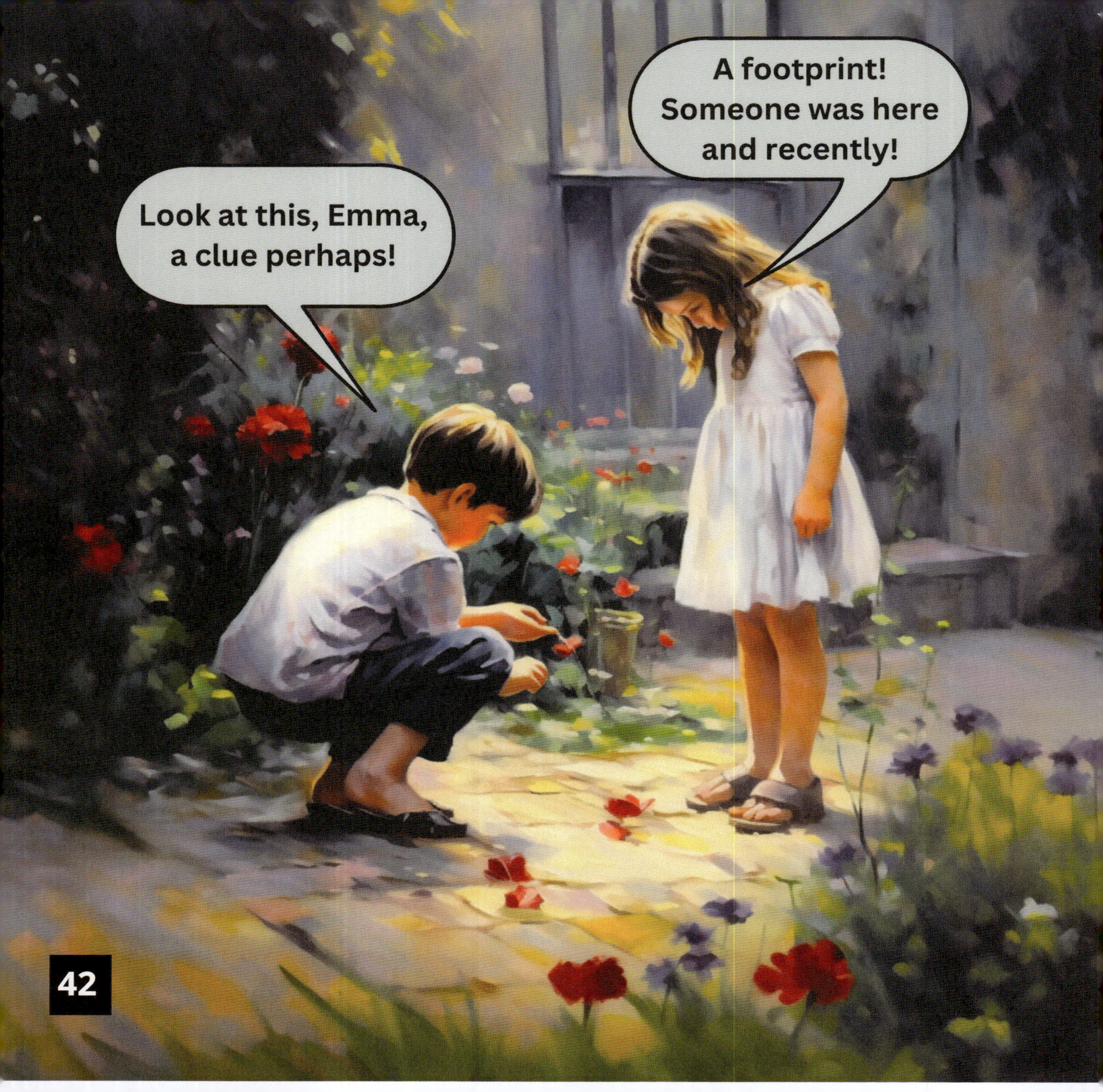
Look at this, Emma, a clue perhaps!
A footprint! Someone was here and recently!

Every painting tells a story, like 'The bridge at Argenteuil'. Can you see the story in the colours and light?

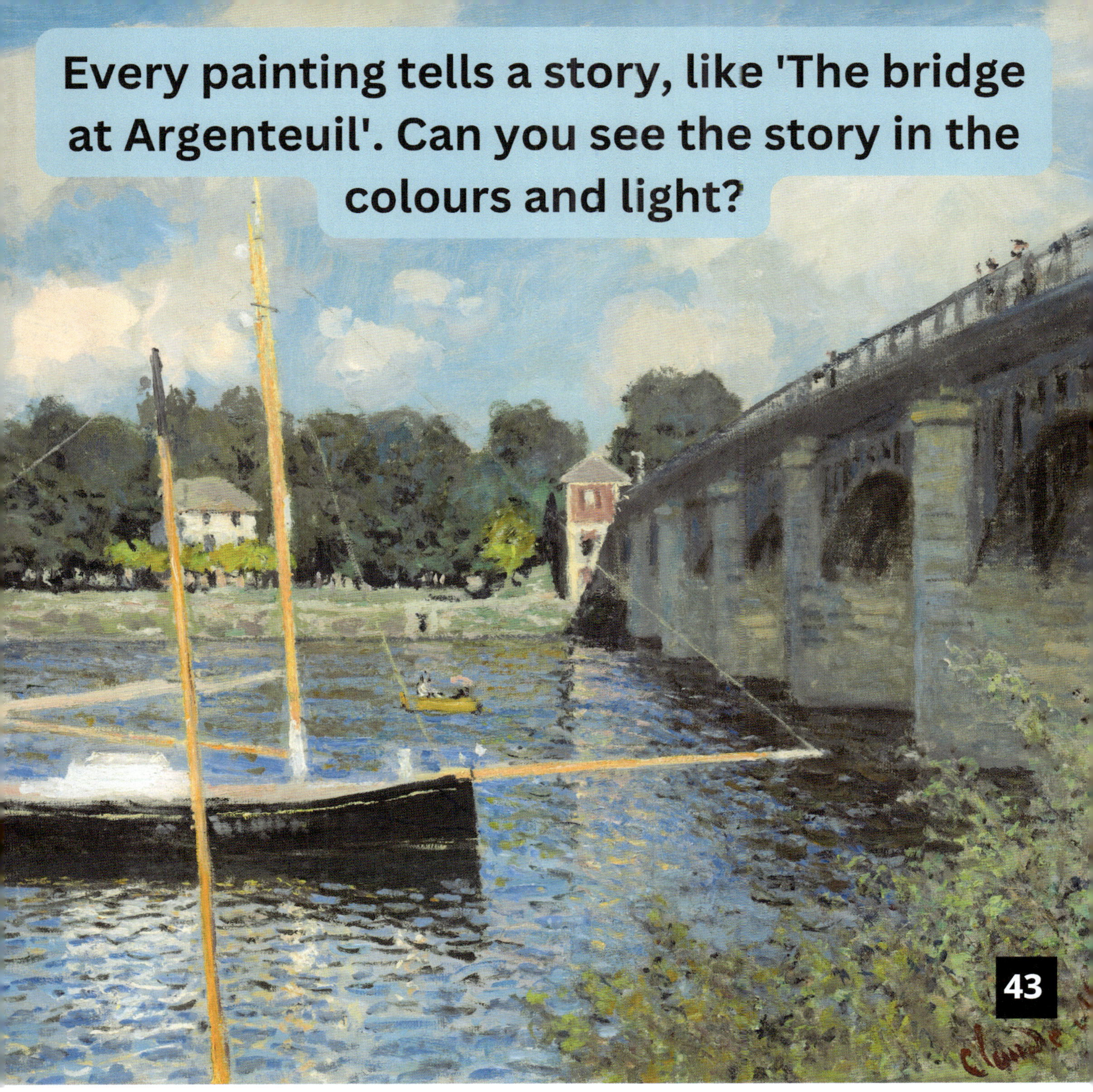

In the studio where secrets hide, Emma and Leo search side by side. Clues in the canvas, in colours they confide, seeking the answers that might coincide.

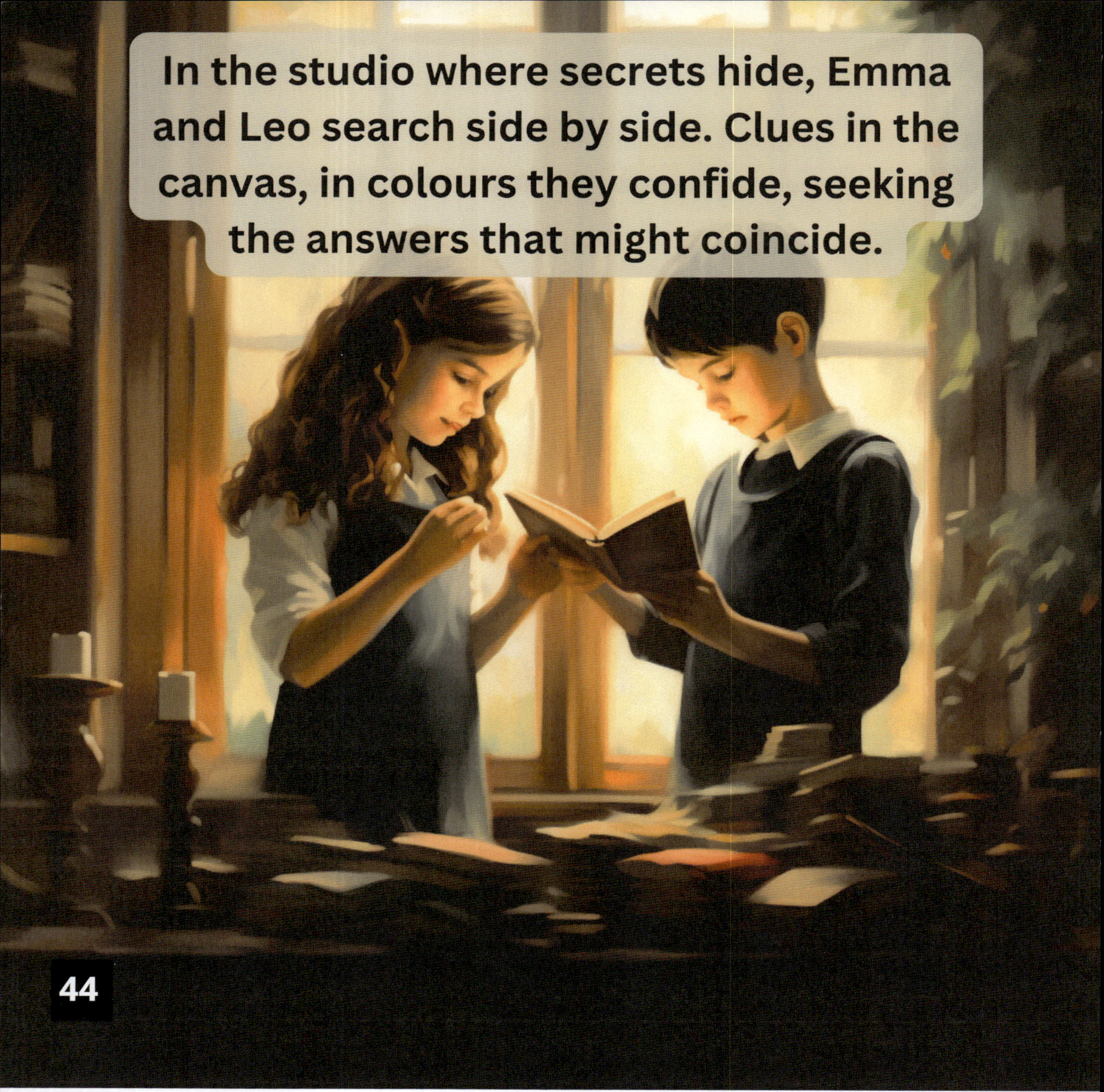

A riddle they find, curious and grand, 'I hide in plain sight, not underhand. Seek where colours blend and stand, where light and shadow playfully land.' Riddle: What am I?

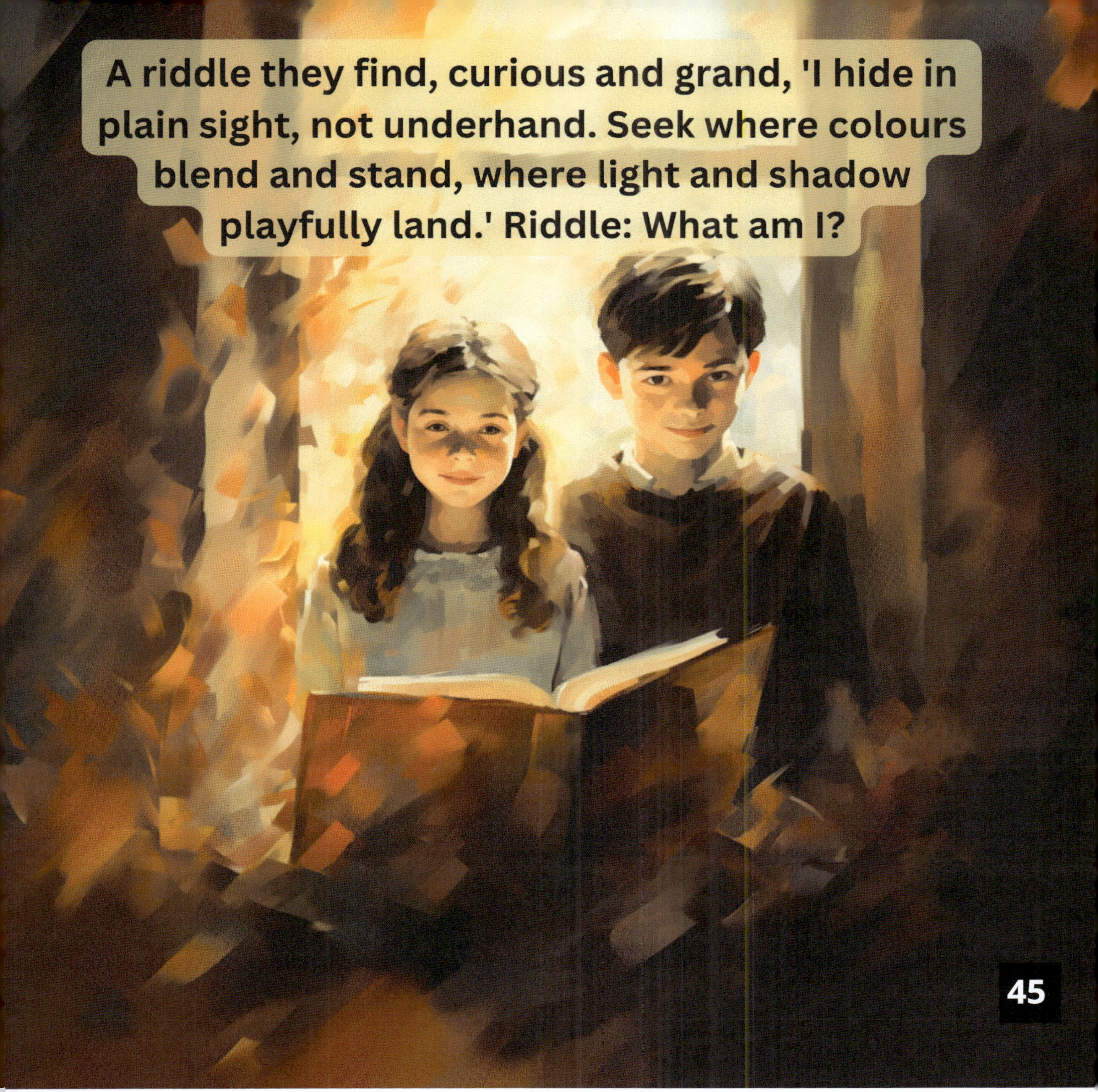

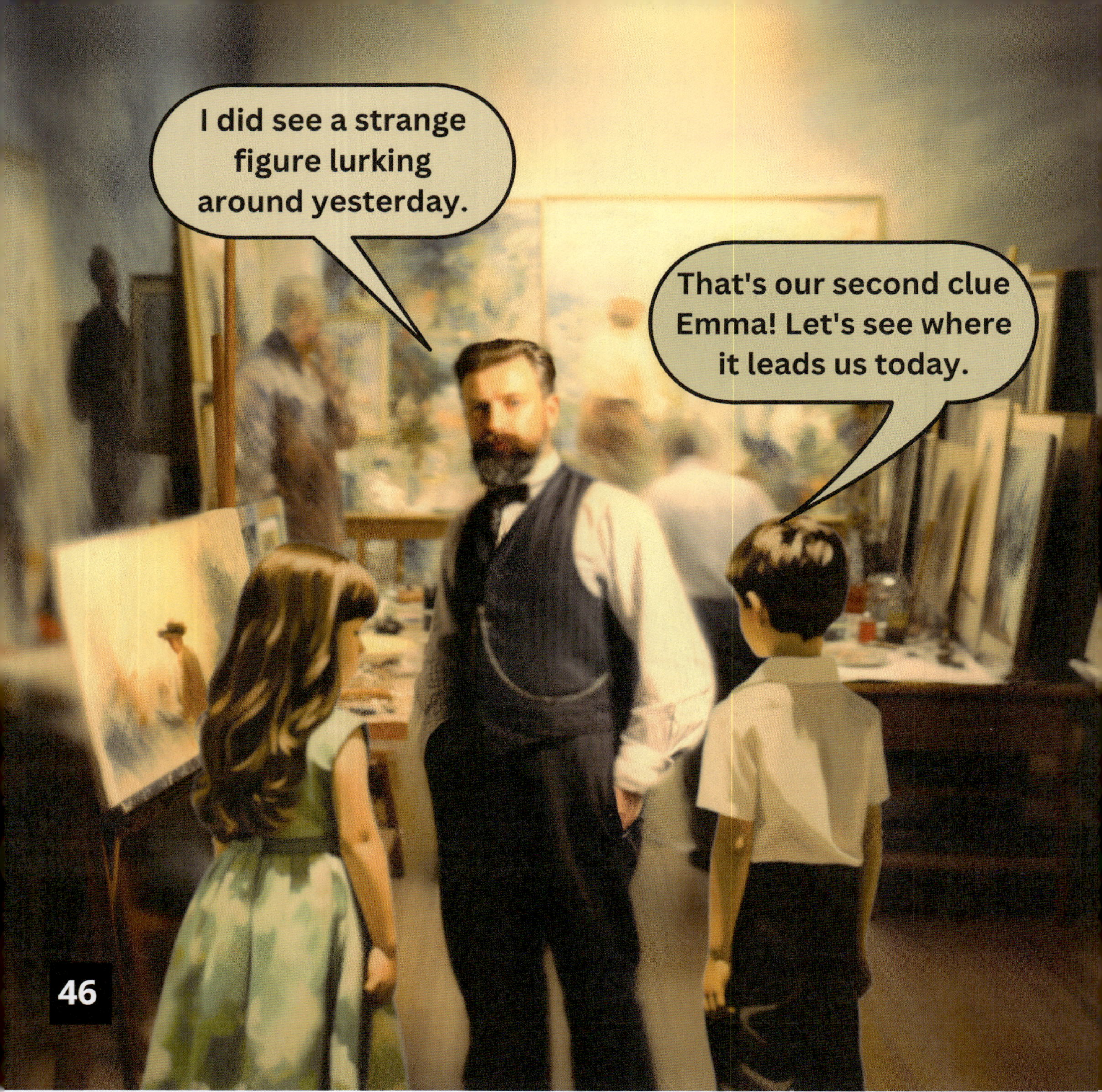
I did see a strange figure lurking around yesterday.
That's our second clue Emma! Let's see where it leads us today.

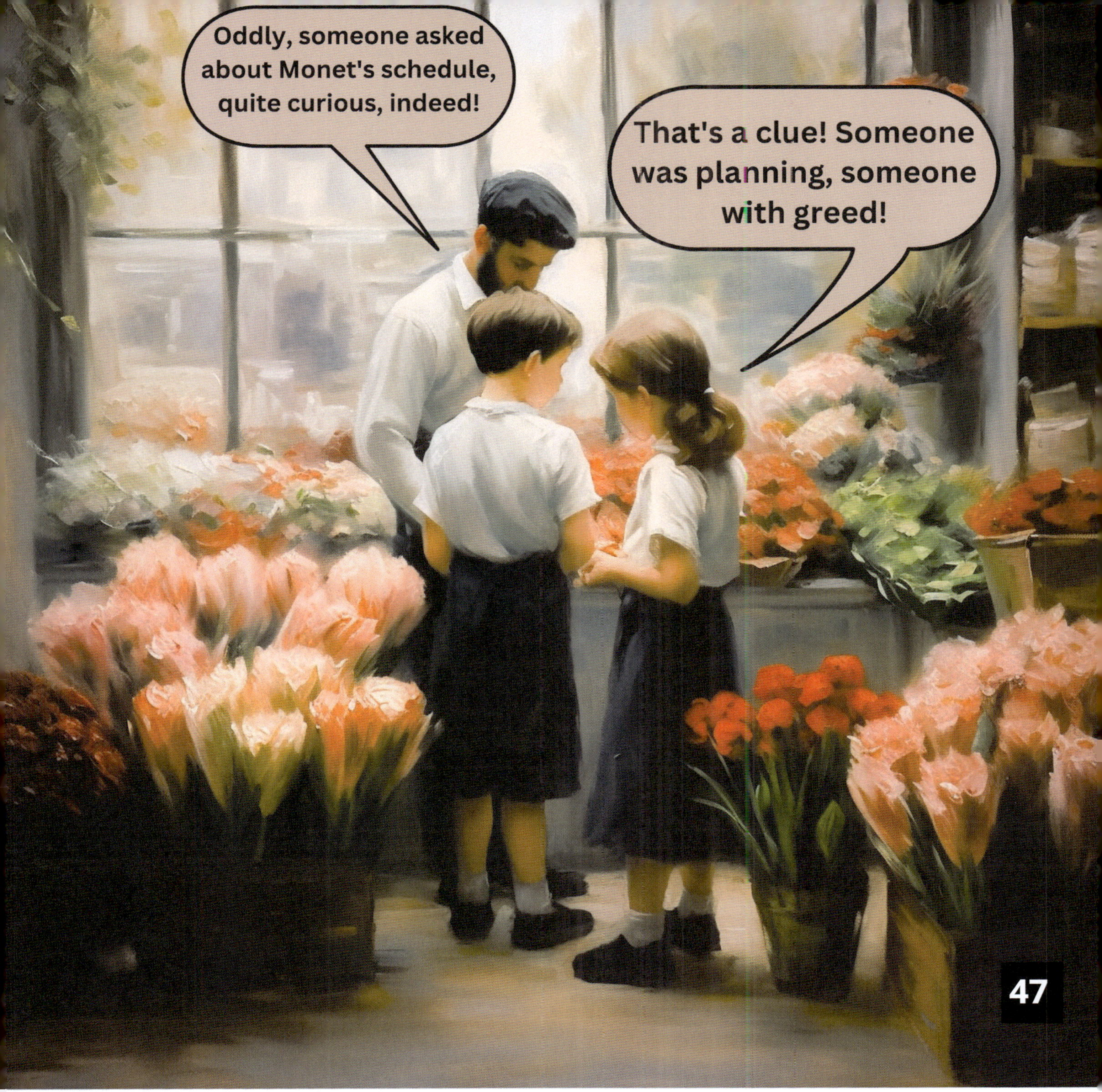
Oddly, someone asked about Monet's schedule, quite curious, indeed!
That's a clue! Someone was planning, someone with greed!

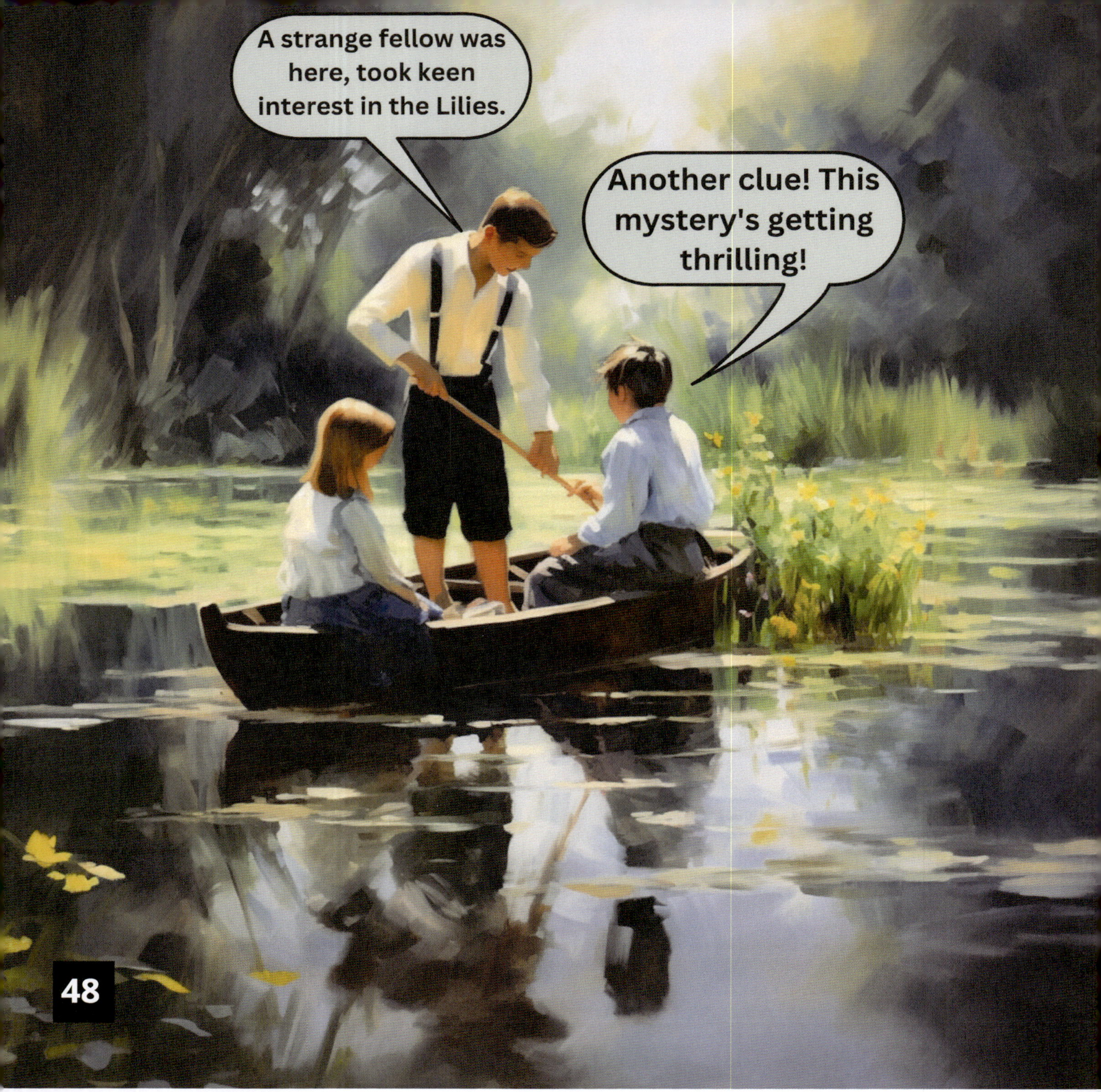
A strange fellow was here, took keen interest in the Lilies.
Another clue! This mystery's getting thrilling!

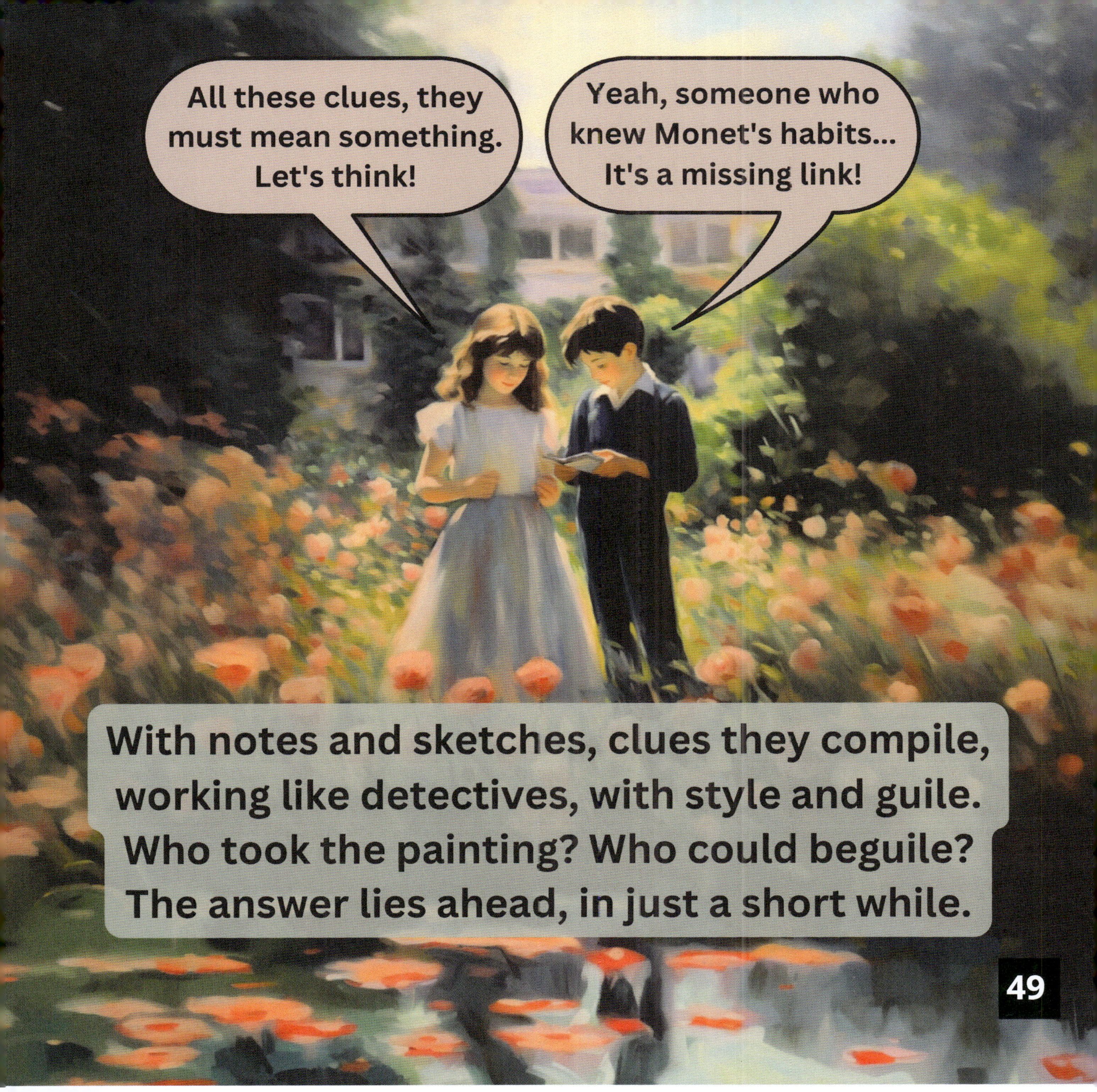

With notes and sketches, clues they compile,
working like detectives, with style and guile.
Who took the painting? Who could beguile?
The answer lies ahead, in just a short while.

"Clues gathered in our detective quest. Footprints, sightings, a riddle's jest. Who is the figure, can you guess? Write your theories, put your mind to the test."

Clue 1: A footprint was found near Monet's studio, indicating a recent visitor.
Clue 2: The statement from Monet's assistant about seeing a stranger lurking near Monet's studio.
Clue 3: The florist's observation about someone inquiring about Monet's schedule.
Clue 4: The fisherman's comment about a strange figure taking an interest in the lilies near the pond.
Clue 5: The mysterious riddle found in the studio, suggests the thief might be someone familiar with the area.

Now it's your turn to be the detective! With the clues we've gathered, who do you think the mysterious figure could be? Use your imagination and the clues below to write your own detective notes or theories.

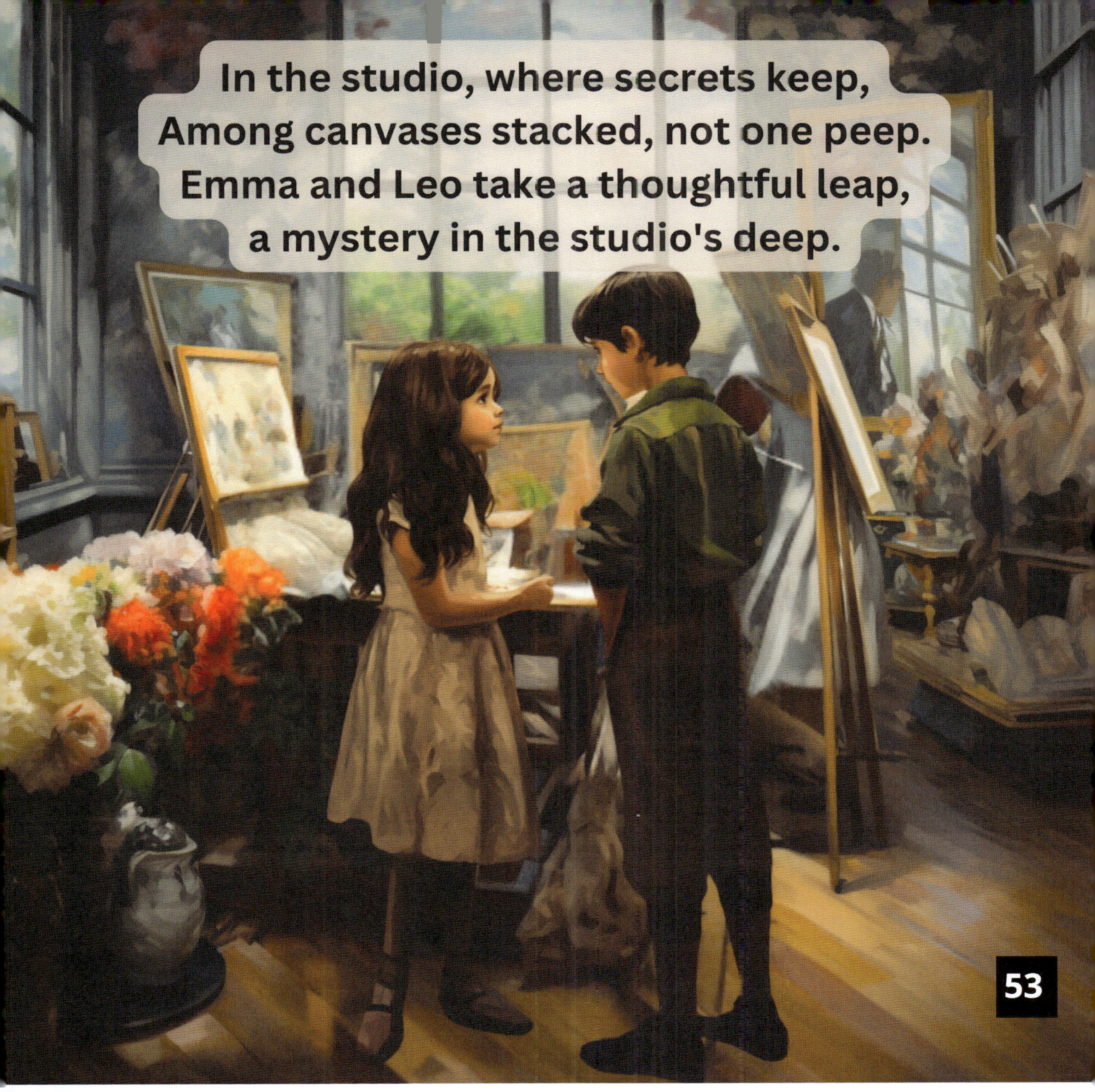

In the studio, where secrets keep,
Among canvases stacked, not one peep.
Emma and Leo take a thoughtful leap,
a mystery in the studio's deep.

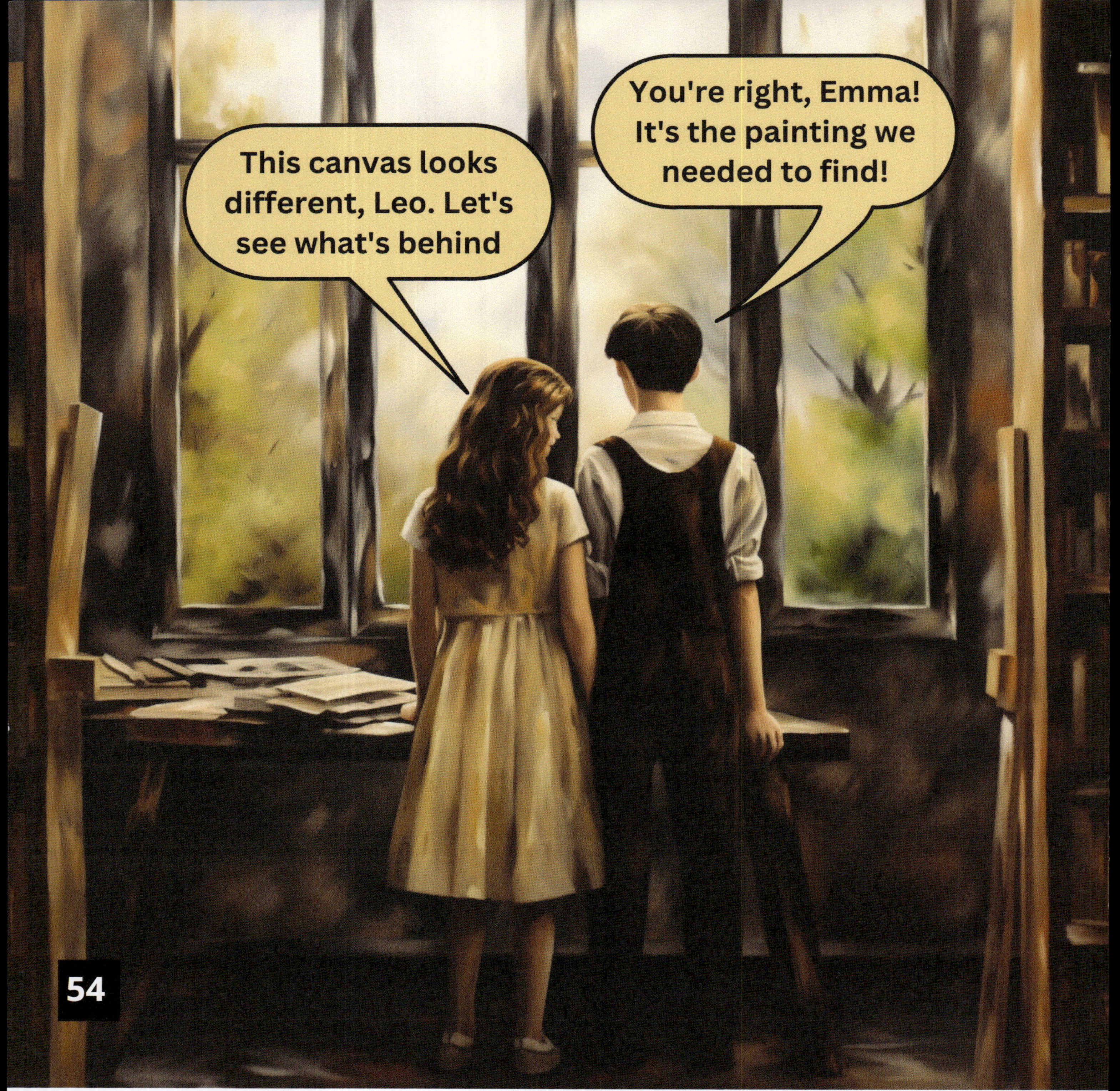
This canvas looks different, Leo. Let's see what's behind
You're right, Emma! It's the painting we needed to find!

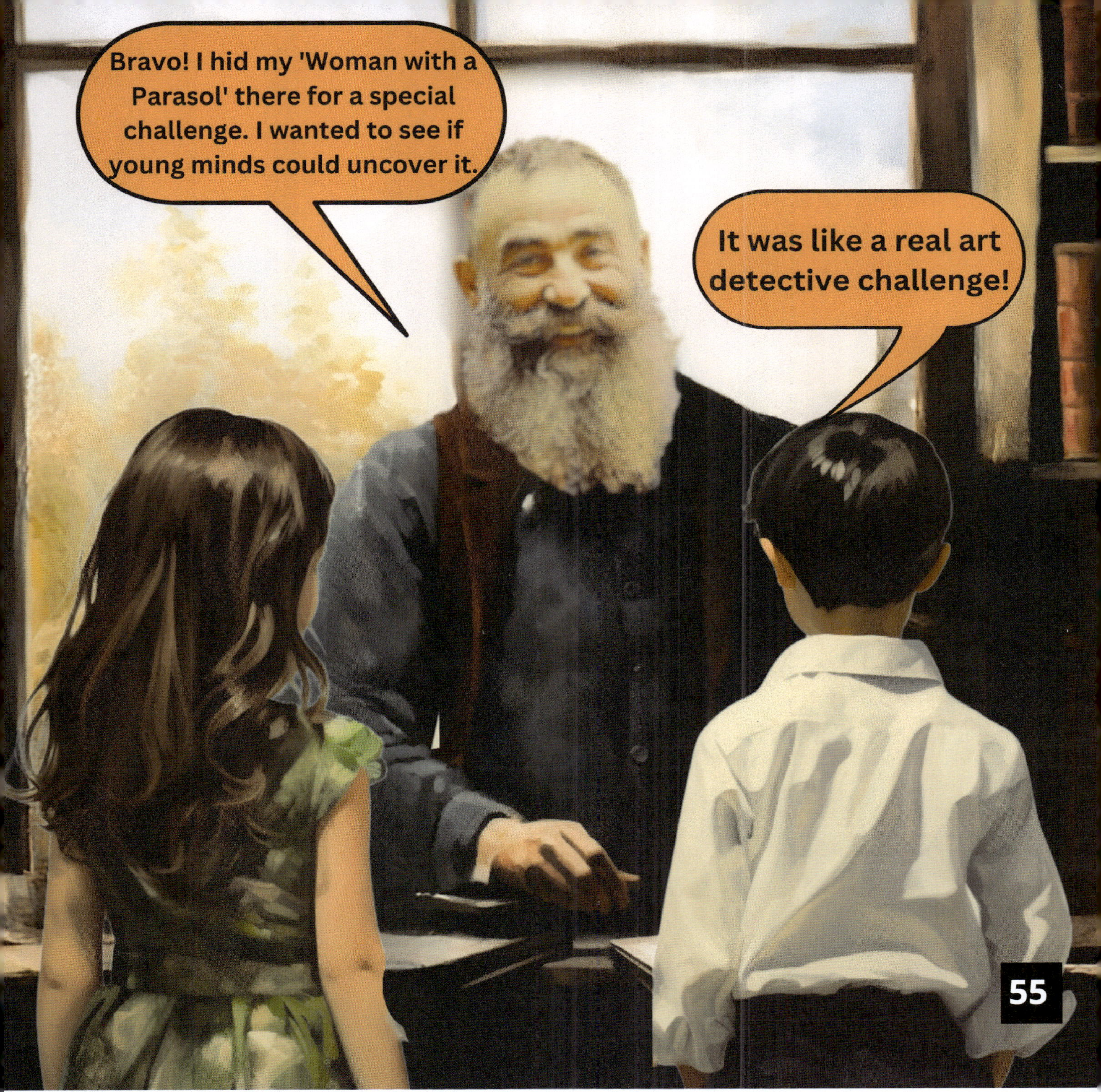
Bravo! I hid my 'Woman with a Parasol' there for a special challenge. I wanted to see if young minds could uncover it.
It was like a real art detective challenge!

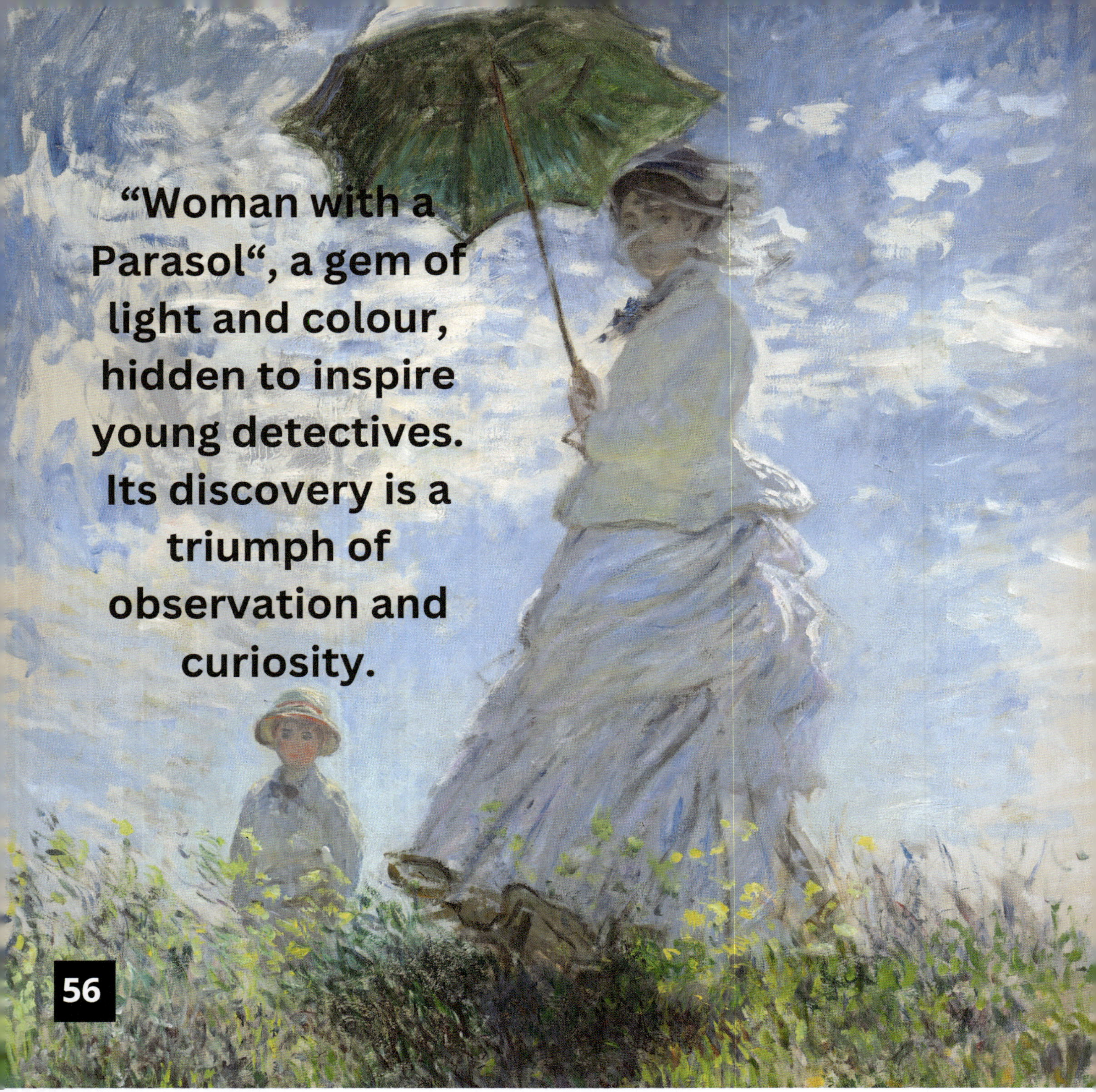

"Woman with a Parasol", a gem of light and colour, hidden to inspire young detectives. Its discovery is a triumph of observation and curiosity.

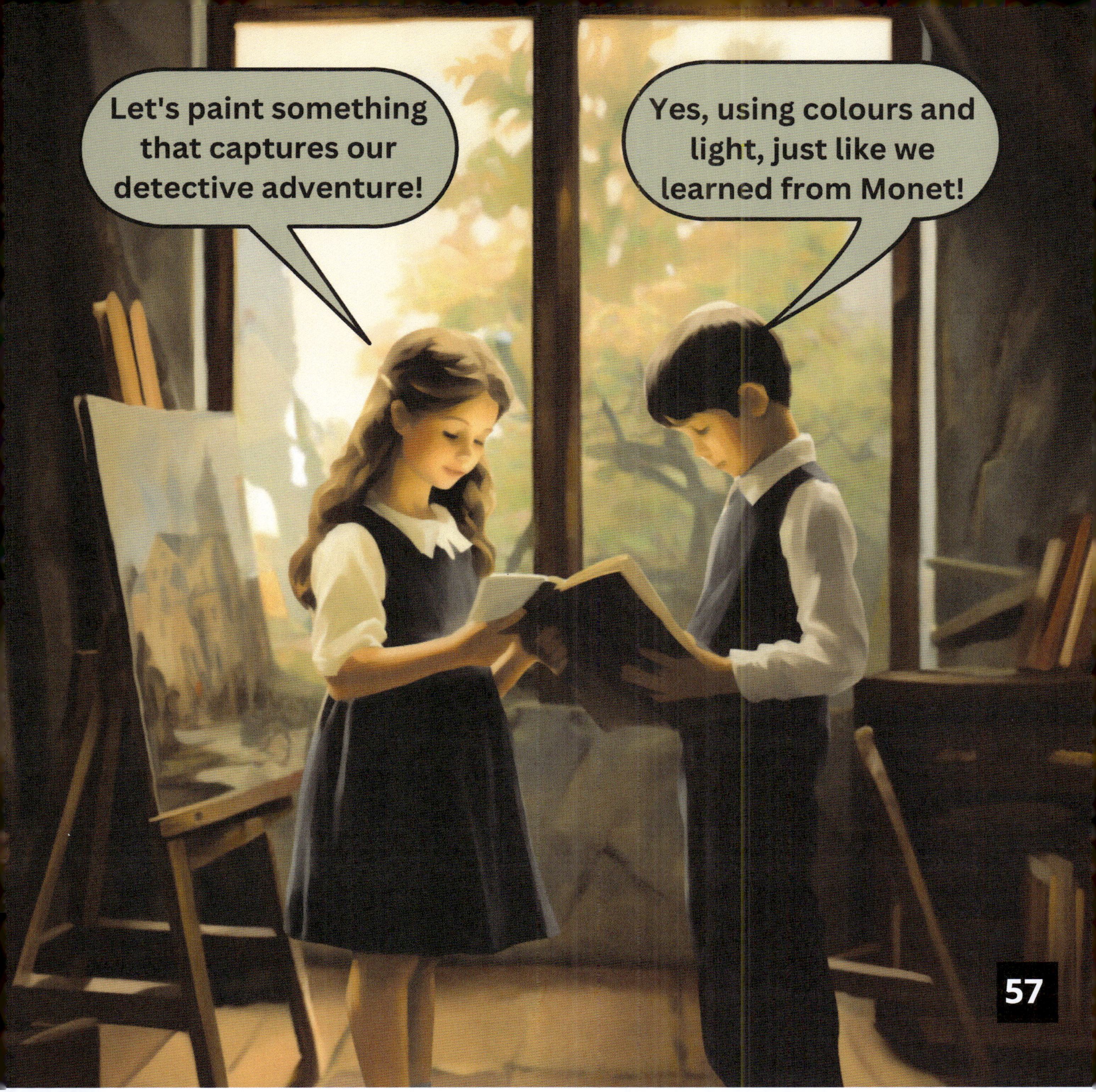
Let's paint something that captures our detective adventure!
Yes, using colours and light, just like we learned from Monet!

Now with colours bold and canvas wide,
reveal your story, don't let it hide.
From detective work to artistic stride,
let your imagination be your guide.

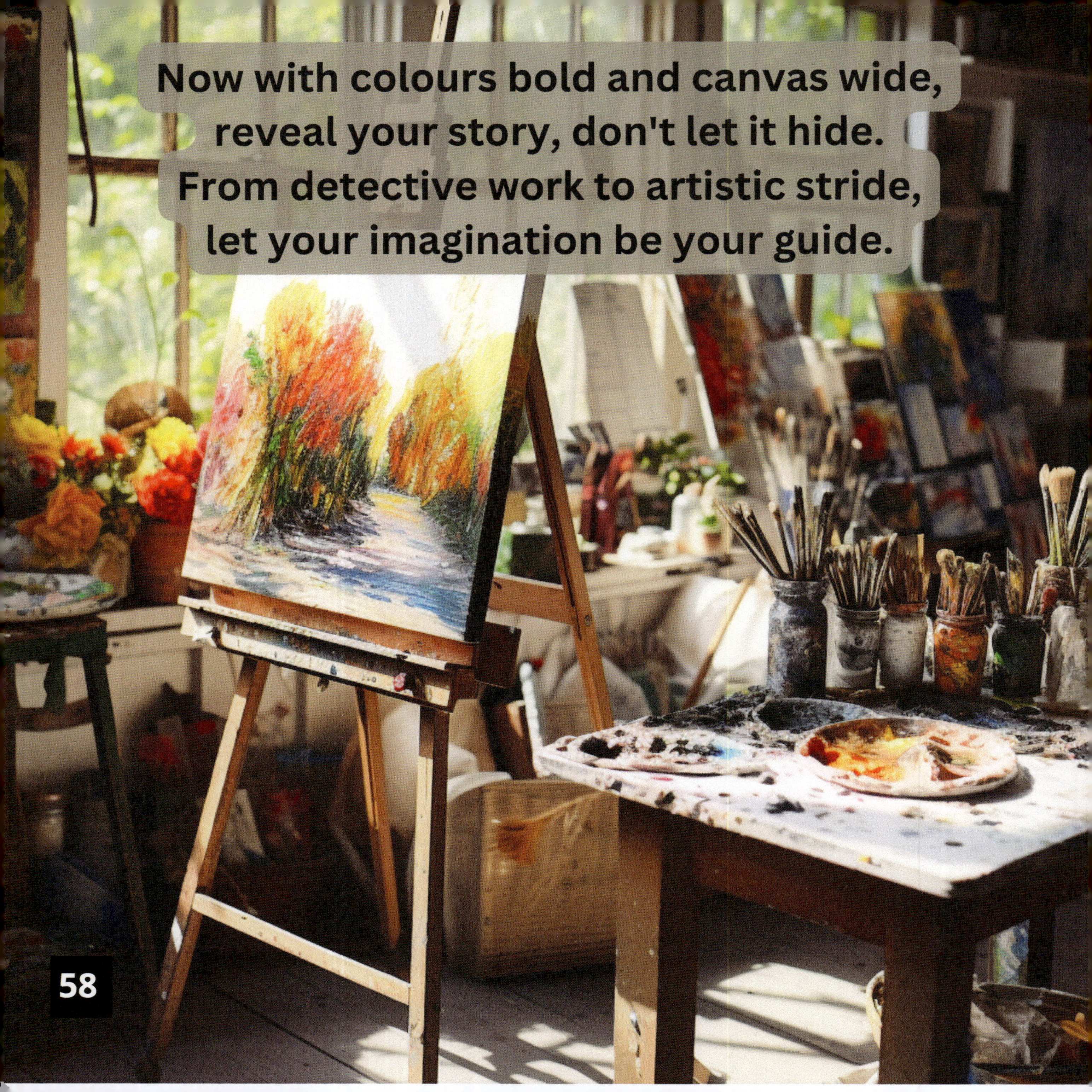

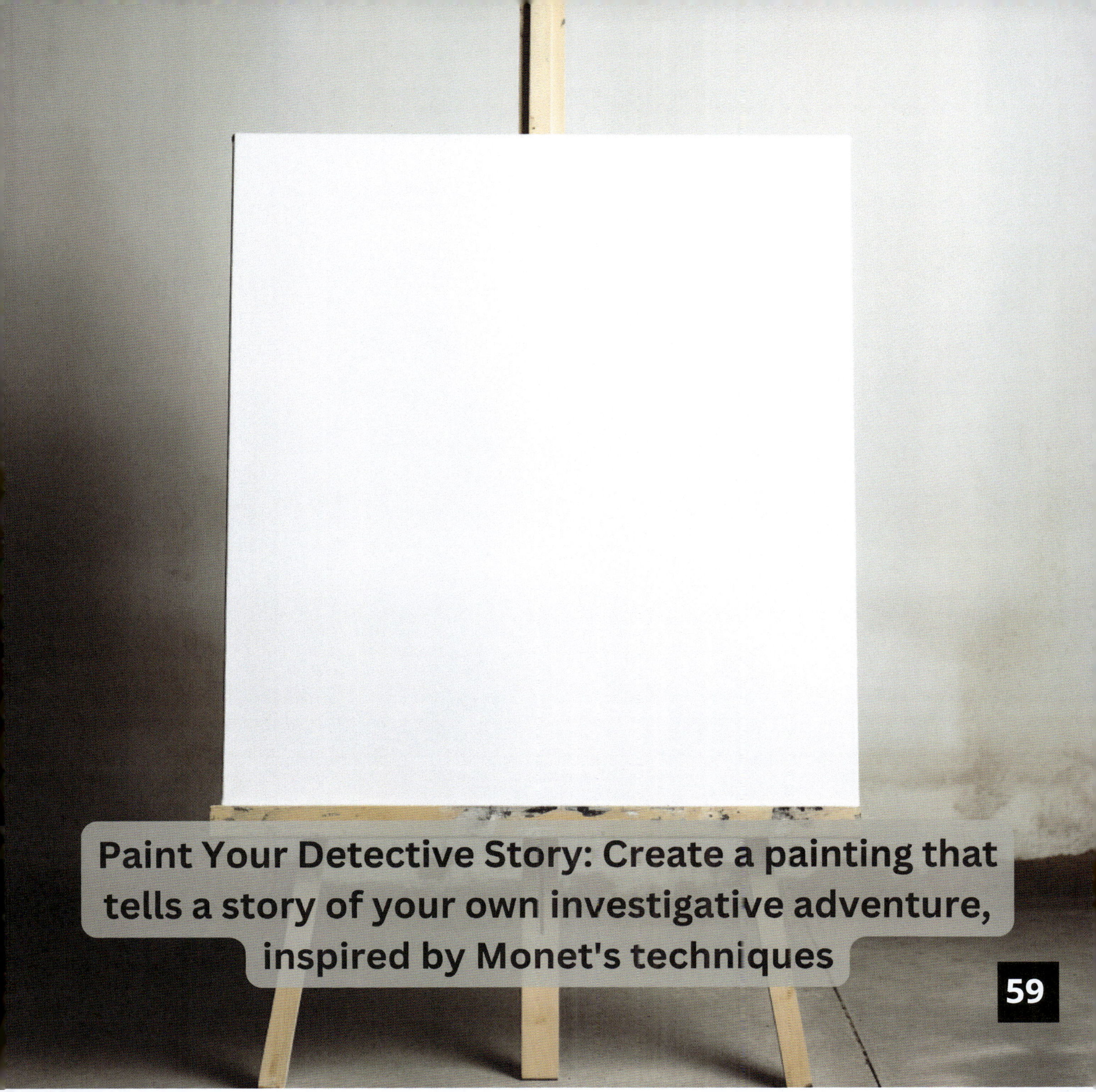

Paint Your Detective Story: Create a painting that tells a story of your own investigative adventure, inspired by Monet's techniques

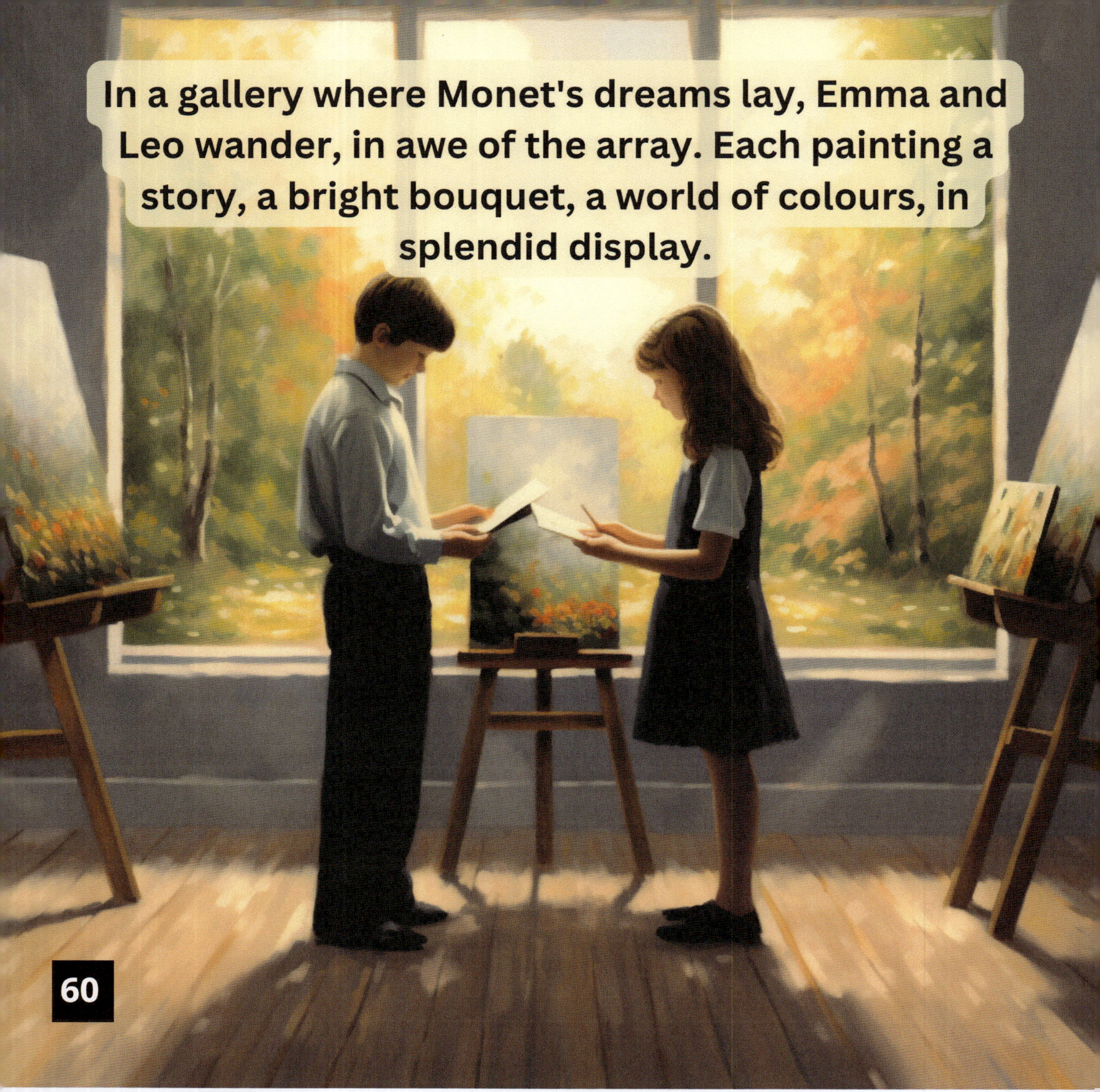

In a gallery where Monet's dreams lay, Emma and Leo wander, in awe of the array. Each painting a story, a bright bouquet, a world of colours, in splendid display.

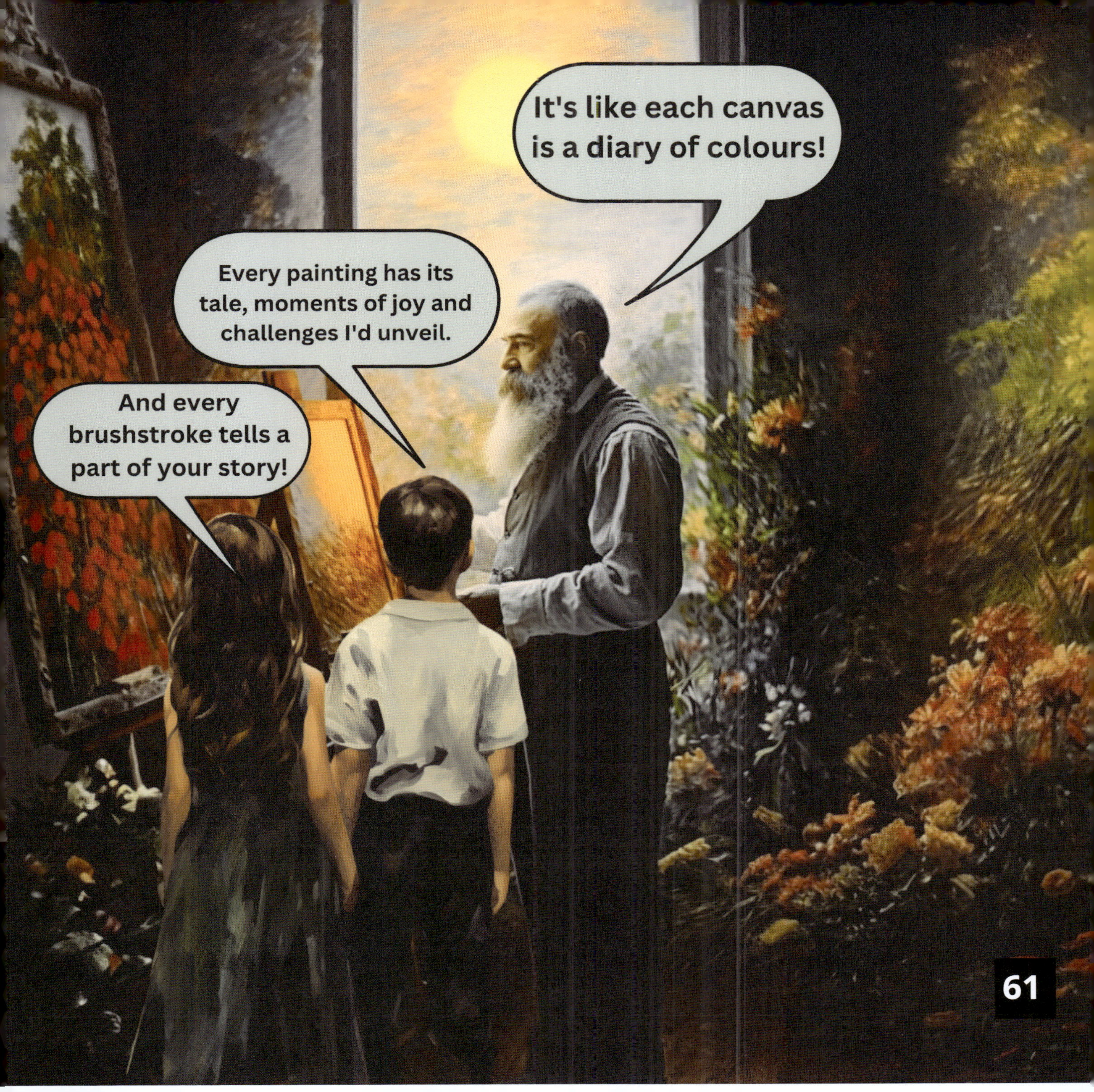

It's like each canvas is a diary of colours!
Every painting has its tale, moments of joy and challenges I'd unveil.
And every brushstroke tells a part of your story!

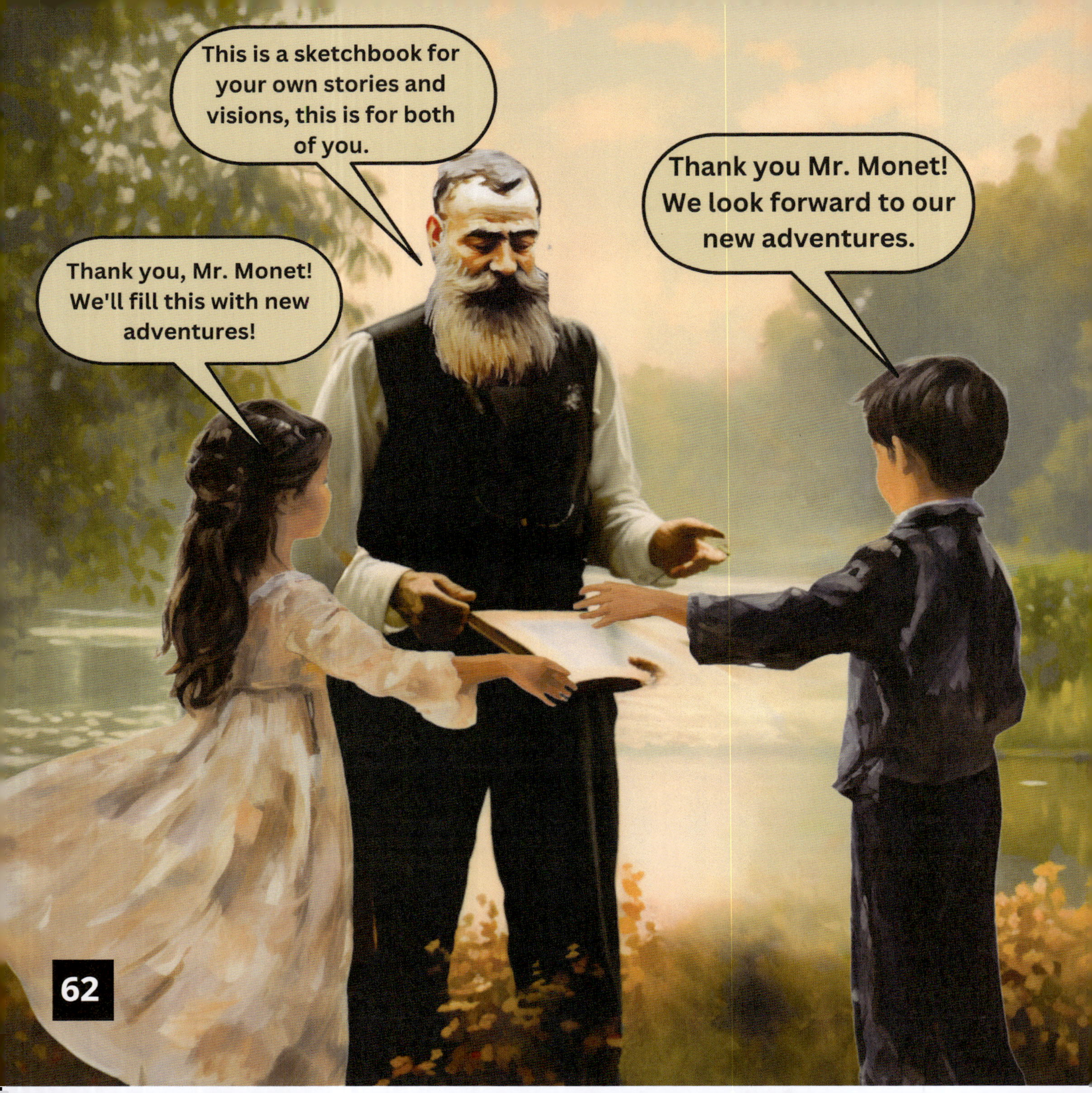
This is a sketchbook for your own stories and visions, this is for both of you.
Thank you, Mr. Monet! We'll fill this with new adventures!
Thank you Mr. Monet! We look forward to our new adventures.

With gift in hand, hearts full of cheer,
Ready for home, they shed no tear.
Inspired by Monet, to them now dear,
Their own artful path, they now steer.

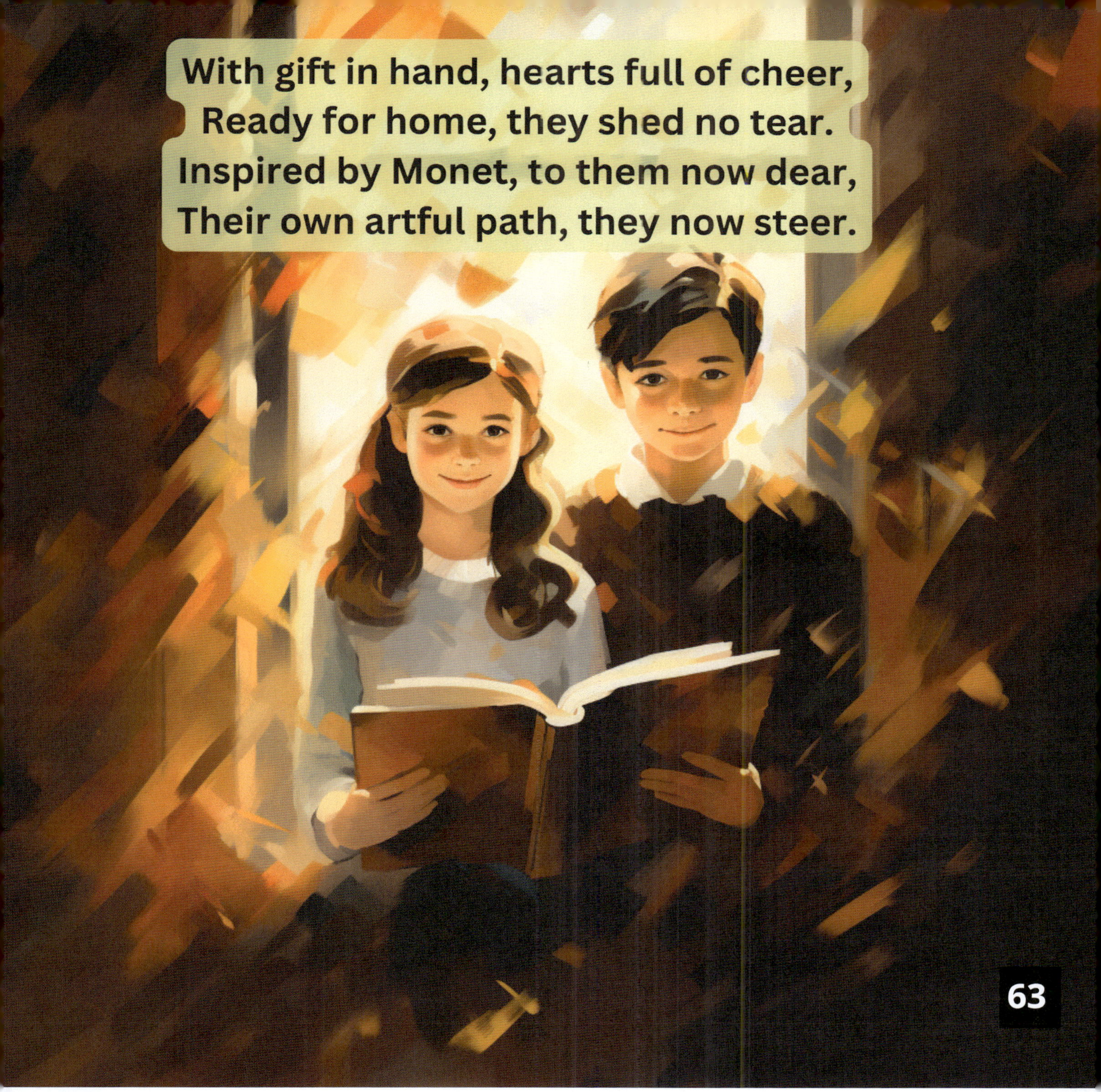

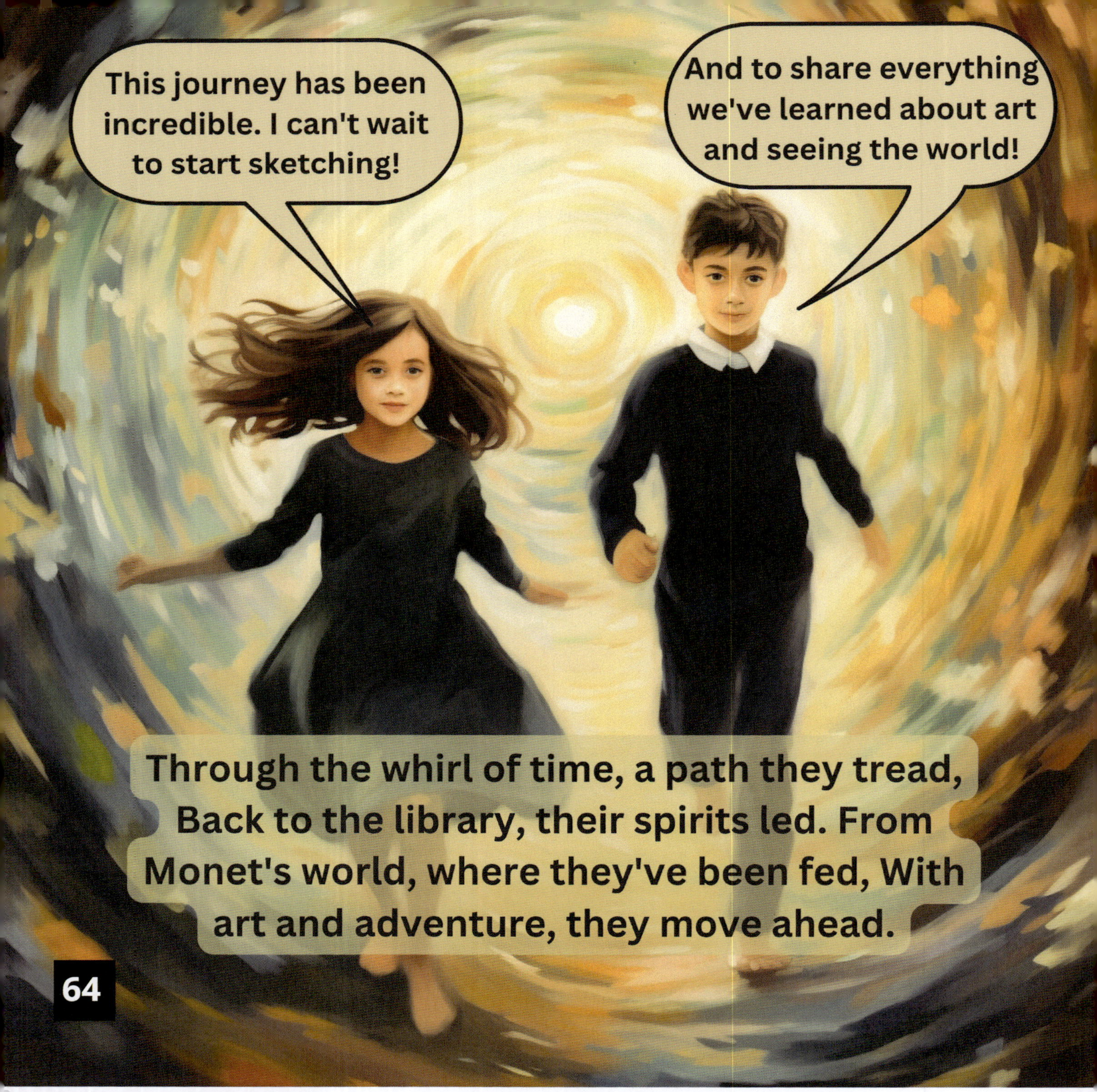

Through the whirl of time, a path they tread, Back to the library, their spirits led. From Monet's world, where they've been fed, With art and adventure, they move ahead.

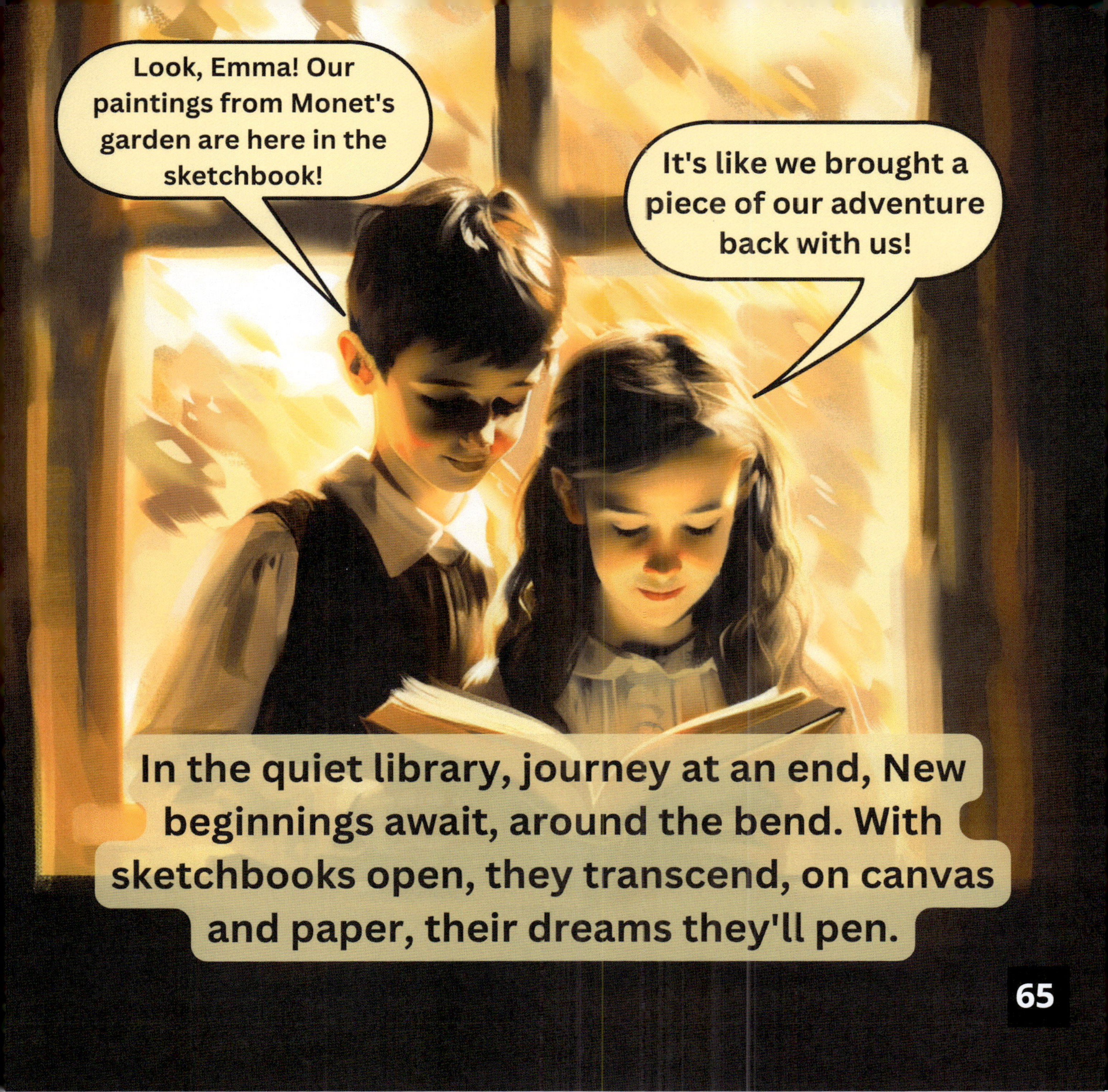
Look, Emma! Our paintings from Monet's garden are here in the sketchbook!
It's like we brought a piece of our adventure back with us!
In the quiet library, journey at an end, New beginnings await, around the bend. With sketchbooks open, they transcend, on canvas and paper, their dreams they'll pen.

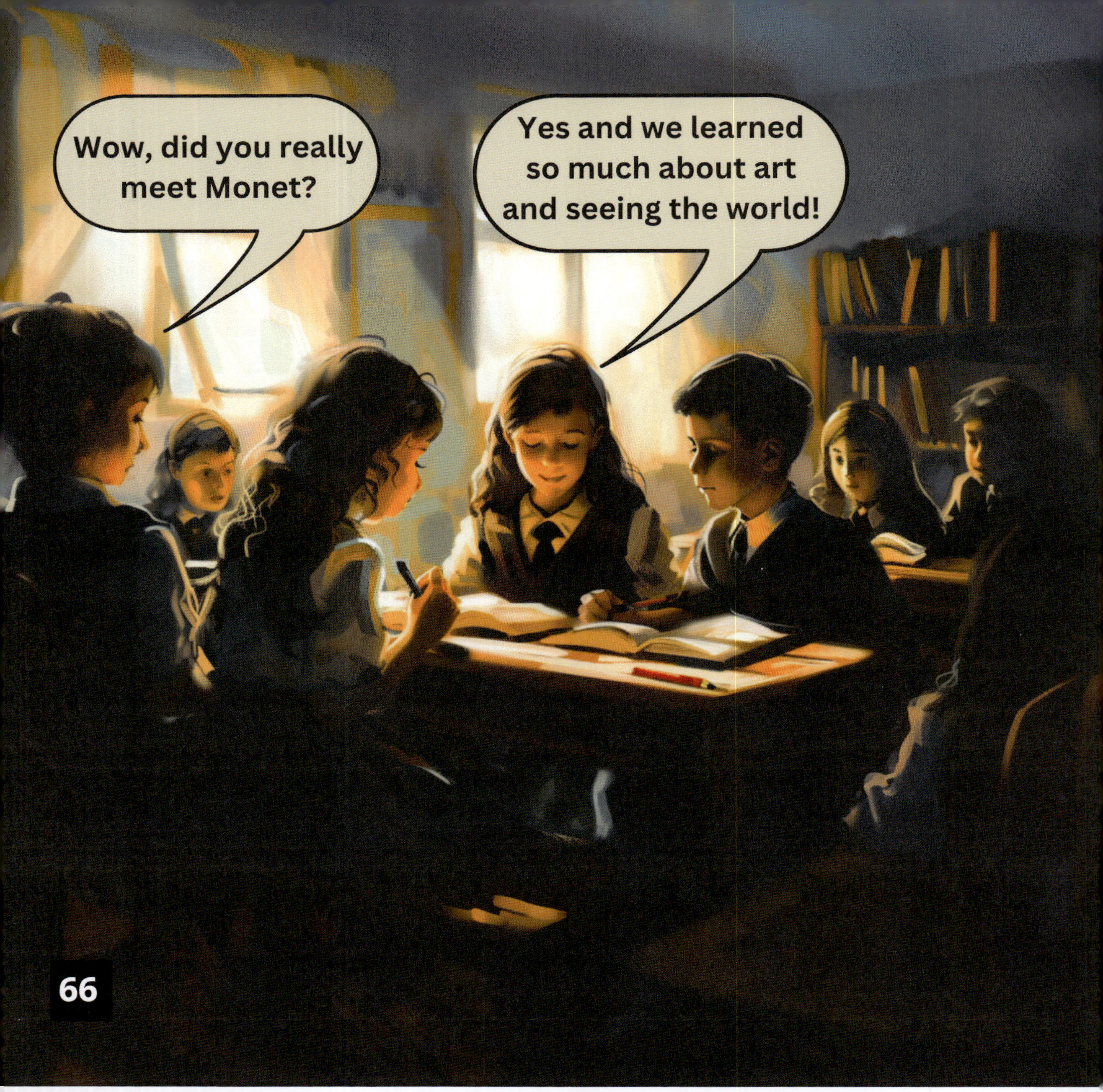
Wow, did you really meet Monet?
Yes and we learned so much about art and seeing the world!

In the classroom, tales they share, of Monet's world, beyond compare. Their friends listen, eyes wide and stare, dreaming of adventures, here and there.

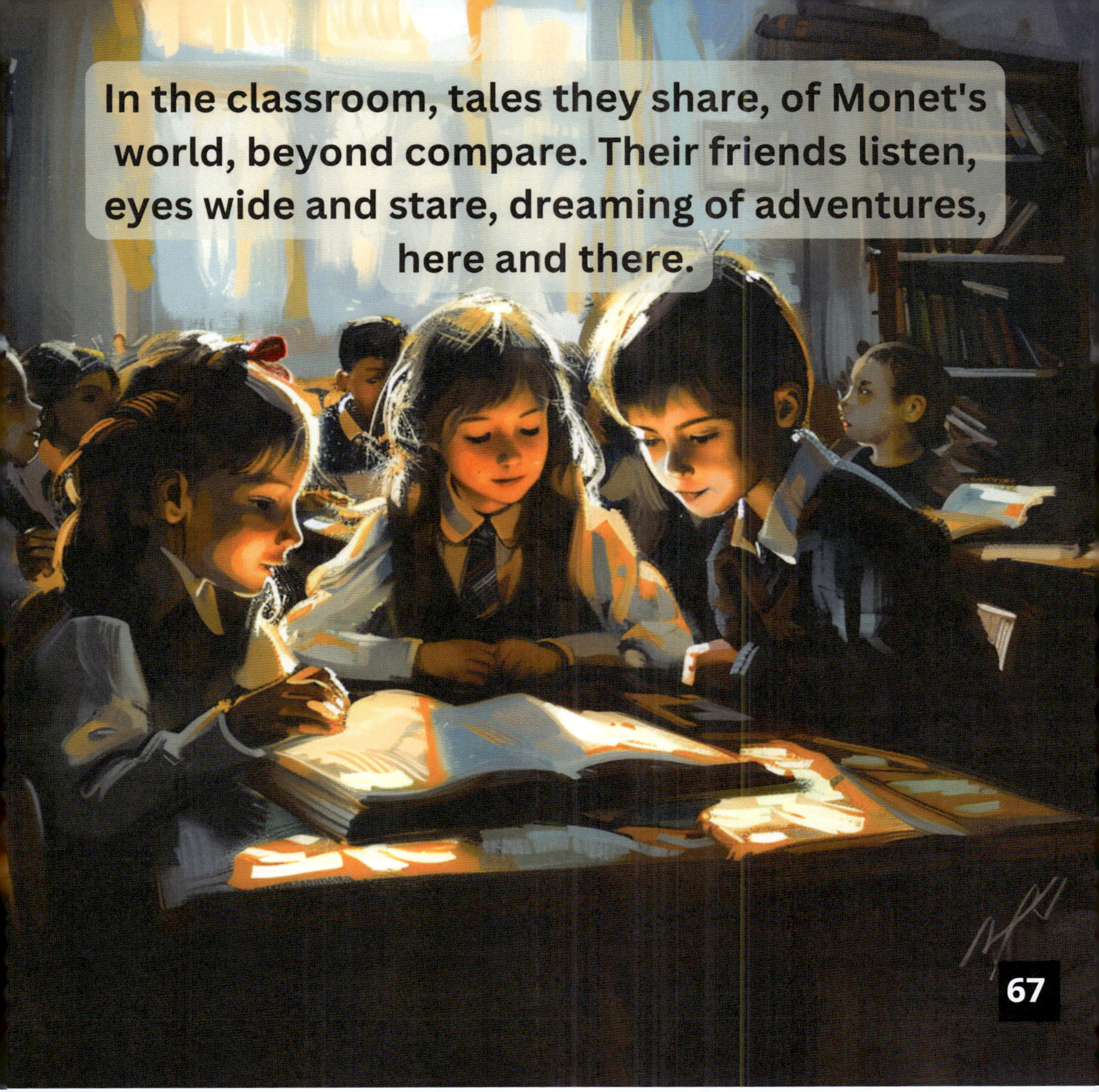

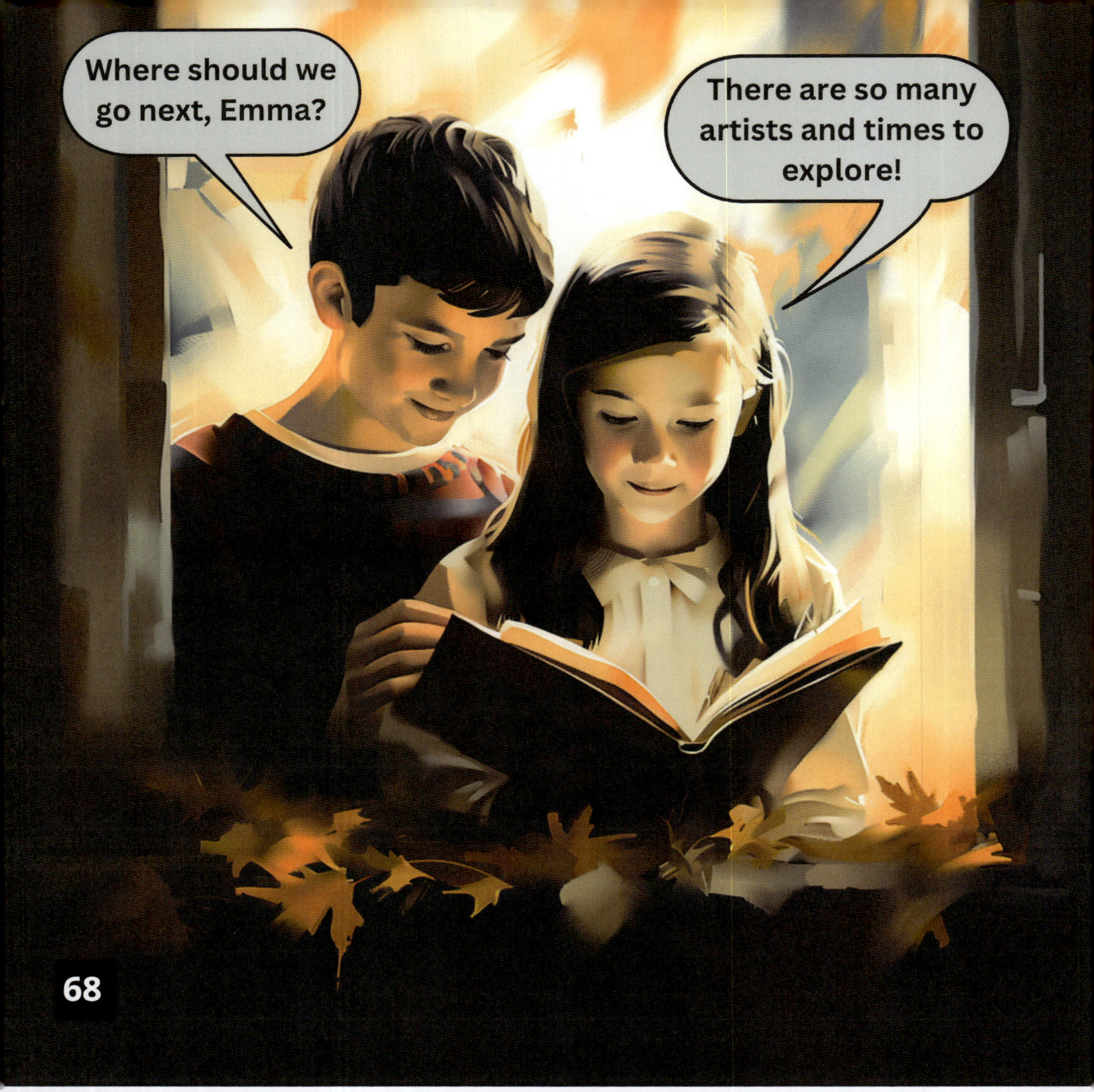
Where should we go next, Emma?
There are so many artists and times to explore!

Now it's your turn, what adventure do you see?
In the pages of history, where would you be?
Draw or write, let your imagination free,
in the world of art, what will your journey be?

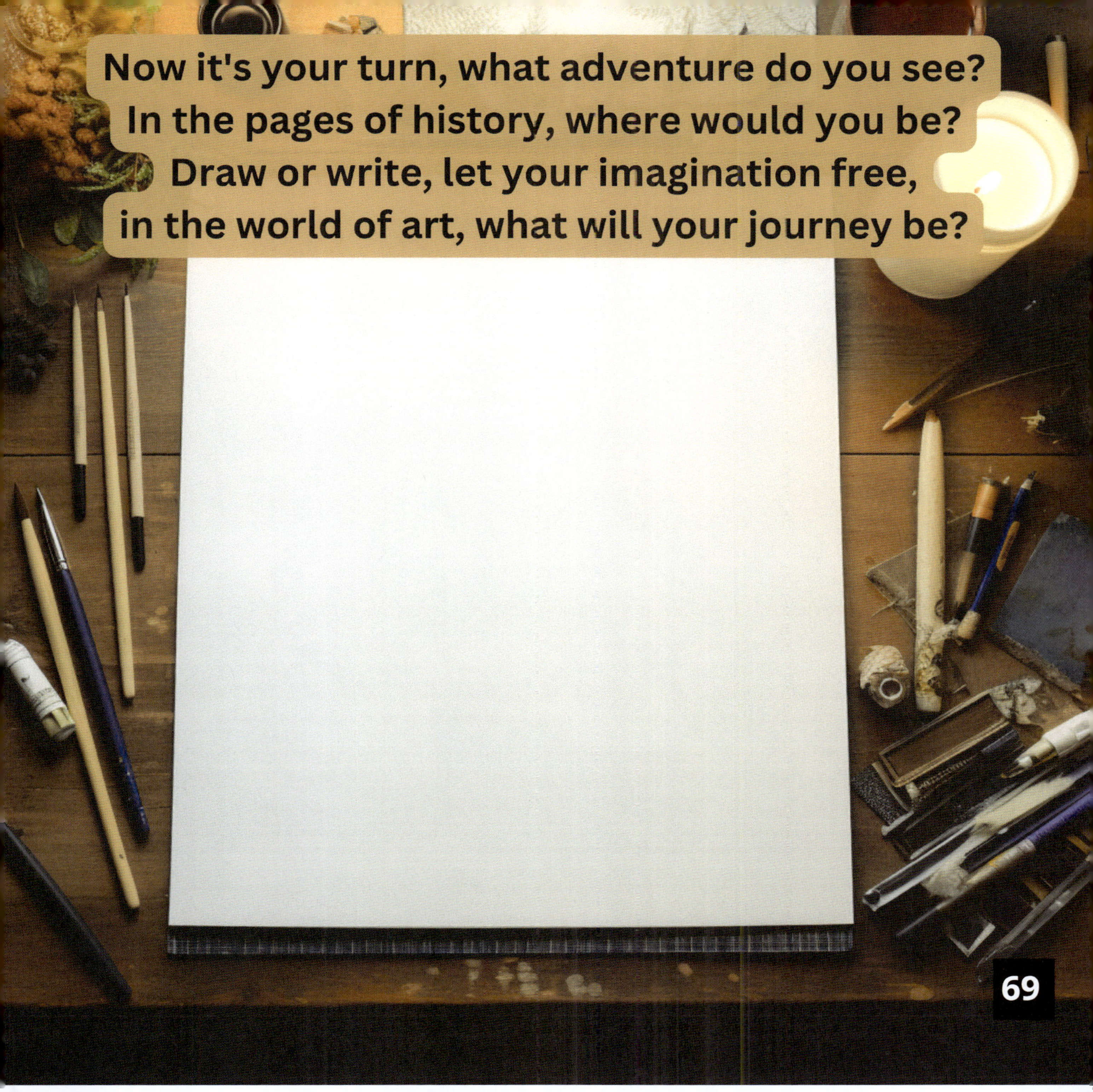

Design Your Adventure: Write or draw your ideas for Emma and Leo's next-time travelling art adventure.

Mario Gabbai combines his extensive Brazilian Jiu-Jitsu background with a passion for educational psychology in his approach to children's literature. His books weave together engaging stories with lessons on resilience and focus, aimed at inspiring young readers to embrace challenges with inner strength.

Writing Philosophy:

Mario is driven by the belief that storytelling is a powerful educational tool. His narratives are filled with adventure, designed to engage children while instilling values such as discipline and perseverance.

Engagement & Community:

With over 25 years in Brazilian Jiu-Jitsu, Mario actively shares his journey, encouraging a balanced life that emphasizes physical well-being and mental resilience.

Claude Monet, a founder of French Impressionist painting, is celebrated for several famous works that beautifully capture the play of light and atmosphere. Some of his most famous paintings include:

1. **Impression, Sunrise (1872)** - This painting, depicting the port of Le Havre, is credited with giving the Impressionist movement its name. It features loose brushwork and a focus on the effects of light and atmosphere rather than detail.

2. **Water Lilies series (1896-1926)** - Monet's series of approximately 250 paintings, focusing on the water lily pond in his garden at Giverny, is one of his most famous and extensive projects. These works vary dramatically in size and palette, capturing the pond's natural beauty across different times of day and seasons.

3. **Woman with a Parasol - Madame Monet and Her Son (1875)** - This painting is a wonderful example of the fleeting effects of light and movement captured on canvas. It depicts his wife and son on a windy summer's day.

4. **The Rouen Cathedral series (1892-1893)** - In this series, Monet painted the facade of the Rouen Cathedral at different times of day and in different light conditions, showing his deep interest in colour and light.

5. **Haystacks (Midday) (1890-1891)** - The Haystacks series is another exploration of the effects of seasonal changes on light and colour, painted at different times of day and in various seasons.

These works are celebrated for their innovation in capturing momentary sensations, as well as for their technical execution and lasting impact on the art world.

Printed in Great Britain
by Amazon

42049677R00043